MW00616766

HELP WANTED

Recruiting, Hiring and Retaining
Exceptional Staff

By Dwayne J. Clark

Edited by Wendy Marsh

Printed by Towner Press
Graphic design by MWW Savitt
Cover Image by Lars Klove

Printed in the United States of America

ISBN 0-9740370-0-1

Dedicated to

Patrick Ian Callahan ("Patau, Uncle Pat")

A working man's man.

July 4, 1933 - June 17, 2000

When people are highly motivated, it's easy to accomplish the impossible. And when they're not, it's impossible to accomplish the easy. So how do we motivate them? Discard the mushroom theory of management — the one that says, keep your employees in the dark and throw a lot of manure on them. If you're going to manage a growing company, you have to concentrate on managing people, not ignoring them.

— Bob Collings

TABLE OF CONTENTS

ACKNOWLEDGEMENTS

With thanks and deep appreciation to the following staff,
friends and companies who helped me with this book:

Irene Olson

Vera Taylor

Polly Miller

Sue Brady

Jeff Turner

Janis Parsley

Derrick Skinner

Jeremy McGinnity

Jim Treadwell and the staff of the Sorrento Hotel

Starbucks Corporation

Costco Corporation

Vision Service Plan

Bartell Drugs

Brown and Haley Candies

Alaska Airlines

Leisure Care Retirement Communities

Sunrise Assisted Living

Emeritus Corporation

Colson/Colson Holiday Management

Alpha Sigma Phi Chapter — University of Washington

Country Meadows of Hershey, Pennsylvania

Economic Development Council of Seattle and King County

Dennis Rockwell, Inglemoor High School DECA Club

Glenn Hammel, Ph.D.

Áegis Assisted Living Staff

Potato Soup

PREFACE

As managers, too often we are disconnected from our line staff. Managers have preferred parking, special benefits, and better salaries. Our assumption is that this gifted group deserves more because they produce more. This is a disastrous business assumption. If you operate a business where you have line staff, there is nothing more important than these employees. We must work along side these employees. We must create venues in which they can communicate. We must constantly look for ways to show appreciation.

If you want to stay in touch with your workforce, don't forget where you came from. I believe this philosophy was instilled in me as a young man growing up in a poor family.

My mother grew up in an affluent household with servants. My grandfather was a senior executive with the British Railroad. He thought nothing of spoiling my mother and her 12 siblings. She grew up like British royalty, living in the lush lands of India. When she got out of school, she joined the British Armed Services and served in World War II. She ended up meeting and marrying my father, an American GI and an Idaho farmer.

She was married to my father for over 20 years before the two divorced and went their separate ways. My mother was left with four children to raise and, basically, no job skills. She did not even get her driver's license until she turned 37. So, she did what came naturally to her: she took a job as a cook — for barely a livable wage. Nevertheless, all four children received a college education and have been successful in their own right.

As the youngest of the four, I was the last to leave the house. When I was in high school, my mother was working very hard to make ends meet. She was sending me to a private school on a church scholarship and trying to get ahead. I was accustomed to our having too little money to buy things that I now take for granted.

I remember coming home one day to see my mother pouring over a stack of bills. The look on her face was a familiar despondent stare and I could tell she wished she had more resources. As I took my jacket off, I asked her what was wrong, already anticipating the answer.

"We are out of money."

I gave some type of sarcastic answer, like, "What's new?"

"No, you don't understand," she said. "We are completely out of money until payday in a week. And we have nothing to eat."

Taking her a little more seriously, I asked what she was planning on doing.

"Well, I have checked the whole house and taken inventory of what food we do have," she said. "We have one large onion, some butter, some cream and some spices."

Trying to make light of the situation, I told my mother that I loved grilled onions, but did not think I could eat them for a week. She was not amused. I will never forget what she told me after that.

"I am going to have to steal some food from work," my mother said. "I won't take anything expensive, but I think with a dozen potatoes we can survive off of potato soup for a week."

You should know that my mother was a very proud and proper British woman. She made sure she taught all of her children good values and ethics. To hear her say she would have to steal some potatoes was difficult for me to believe. However, I agreed it was the only solution. My mother vowed that we would pay the restaurant back — which she did, even adding some potatoes beyond reimbursement. Nevertheless, we lived off potato soup for a week, and I'll never forget it.

During that week, my mom and I would talk about what I wanted to do when I grew up. I would throw out crazy ideas. One night, as we sipped our soup, she stopped me as I was in mid-brainstorm. She said, "Dwayne, no matter what you do, don't ever forget where you came from. Do not ever forget that you had to eat potato soup for a week. If you ever have people that work for you, realize that sometimes things in life may not go right, and they will need your help. Sometimes they may not ask you, but you will notice something is wrong by the way that they act. Be there for your employees, and they will always be there for you."

I have read hundreds of business books, but I do not think I have heard wiser words than those of my mother's that night. Today, I have a plaque on my office wall with those two simple words: "Potato Soup." It is a constant reminder to me of my struggles as well as those my staff members go through every day. The only difference is that now I have the power to effect change in their lives.

As managers, we can bathe in the spoils of our success, losing touch with the true heroes who make American businesses a success — the line staff worker. Stay in touch, stay in tune and you'll stay in business.

Introduction

As employers, we are faced with a monumental business concern: finding and keeping qualified and motivated staff for our line positions. Whether you operate a restaurant in Hackensack, New Jersey, or an assisted living senior community in Walla Walla, Washington, your business' long-term financial well-being is threatened by the competition for a shrinking skilled employee pool.

Companies that have not had a problem recruiting or retaining employees should start to brace themselves. If you have a reputation for attracting good staff there is good news and bad news. The good news is it helps in your recruiting efforts for new employees. The bad news is that because of the lack of employees on the market your company will be a primary target from which your competitors can harvest employees. This book does not just focus on the problem. It offers creative insights and solutions. Although the book primarily uses examples gained from the experiences of those in long-term care and senior housing, its lessons are equally applicable to other industry segments.

If this dilemma is already causing you high anxiety, you're not alone, as has been documented by the Grant Thornton Business Owners Council. Their poll of more then 400 business owners and senior executives indicated 83 percent consider employee talent to a be a vital issue, trailing only to customer service as a key factor in gaining a competitive advantage in the workplace. However, only a startling 41 percent of those polled rate themselves as being more effective than their competitors in successfully attracting and retaining employees.

Unemployment numbers continue to hover around the 5 percent mark. Even if our economy worsens, the demand for entry level line staff is increasingly competitive. Demographic trends show that in the next 10 years, employers could face an increase in older workers and a marked decrease in younger workers.

Employee turnover is expensive in a number of ways. The National Association for Priority Leadership estimates the cost of losing an employee can run from 150 percent to 300 percent of annual compensation. This means if you lose just three employees a year with an average annual salary of $30,000, the associated costs can run from $135,000 to $270,000 annually.

Recently, a Princeton, New Jersey consulting company looked at financial costs associated with recruitment and retention. The study's author, Sibson and Company, put the cost of turnover in perspective. For example, the study found that turnover of sales clerks in specialty retail stores is 97 percent nationwide. The study concluded that this turnover costs the industry 50 percent of its yearly earnings. Looking at this in another way, it means that to recoup the cost of losing one sales clerk, a clothing store must sell 2,984 pairs of khaki pants at $35 each, assuming a profit margin of 10 percent.

The value of work can't be measured in dollars alone. There's also the sense of dignity and self-worth that comes from being able to provide for ourselves and our families. But employees will become frustrated when a full-time job will purchase only a part-time life. It's our responsibility as employers to pay a living wage, however, it would be shortsighted to not realize the other elements of satisfaction employees look for in a job. To not be realistic about these other factors suggests a lessening of the value that we as a society place on work, family and the community.

Even if you feel you have a company culture that is ahead of the game in relation to staff retention through pay and benefits, you may not be in touch with your employees. An article in Office.com's online newsletter indicates that on-the-job time has increased for an employee by 163 hours in a given year over the last two decades. At the same time, leisure time for Americans has declined by one-third. Today, workers are willing to sacrifice twice as much pay as their counterparts were seven years ago to achieve more of a balance between their work and their personal life.

Additionally, 55 percent of the 18- to 34-year-olds say the option of taking extended leaves or sabbaticals is a key workplace benefit. Companies have found that they can increase productivity, revenue, or both by 20 percent by simply implementing a work/life-balance program for staff.

Some of the best insights this book has to offer were collected through interviews with service workers — not just about benefits and salary preferences, but also about the type of treatment they value. What is important to employees in picking a company culture? What little "retention nuggets" will gain their loyalty to your company? The interviews reflect a variety of industries from the hotel to the healthcare sector and reveal vital information for employers.

This book will help you develop a strategy to assist you in finding and keeping the best staff, one that will afford you a significant advantage over your competitors. Employers have had to become professional interviewers. This book describes how to get the most out of the interviews and obtain information legally through unconventional methods. It will also provide you with great ideas on how to wisely use your recruiting dollars as well as help your managers format and develop a quarterly recruiting plan.

Please realize that turnover does not only cost you in recruiting time, it costs you in efficiency, customer service and regulatory penalties. The business of keeping staff is the number one business issue of the 21st century.

The High Cost of Turnover

CHAPTER 1

It's no secret that it's an employees' market. Even with economic uncertainties, more people who want to work do work, and the pool of potential entry-level employees is low. That means that employers have to offer incentives to attract and retain employees.

Add to this the fact that the workforce is aging. The number of young adults will be reduced sharply over the next several years, while the number of those aged 55 to 64 will double between now and 2020. The graying of the U.S. population will put increasing pressure on your hiring and employee retention efforts. Older workers will be a significant resource. With a continuing labor shortage, you should be looking for all the people you can find to get on board.

Just as significant as the above statistics are the costs and impact associated with an employee who leaves your company. Calculating the cost of turnover in any organization will vary, but you should remember that the costs of time and lost productivity are no less important or real than the costs associated with paying cash to vendors for services such as advertising or temporary staff. These are all very real costs to you, the employer. As noted in the "Introduction" of this book, these calculations will easily reach 150 percent of the employee's annual compensation figure. The cost will be significantly higher for managerial and sales positions.

It may seem hard to believe, but consider just the minimal costs listed below.

Calculate the cost of:

- a temporary employee or the cost of existing employees performing the vacant job as well as their own. Who will pick up the work, whose work will suffer, what departmental deadlines will not be met or will be delivered late?

- lost productivity at a minimum of 50 percent of the person's compensation and benefits for each week the position is vacant, even if there are people performing the work.

- the administrative costs of stopping payroll, benefit deductions, COBRA notification and administration, and various forms needed to process a resigning employee.

- training that your company has invested in the exiting employee. Include internal training, external programs and licenses or certifications.

- unemployment insurance premiums as well as the time spent to prepare for an unemployment hearing, or the cost paid to an attorney to handle the claim process on your behalf.

The number of young adults will be reduced sharply over the next several years, while the number of those aged 55 to 64 will double between now and 2020. The graying of the U.S. population will put increasing pressure on your hiring and employee retention efforts.

- recruiting advertisements (from a $200 classified to a $5,000 or more display advertisement).

- implementing a sourcing strategy, reviewing candidates' backgrounds, conducting interviews and conducting reference checks.

- drug screens, educational and criminal background checks and other reference checks.
- the person(s) conducting the training.
- various training materials needed including company or product manuals, computer or other technology equipment used in the delivery of training.
- supervisory time spent in assigning, explaining and reviewing work assignments and output.
- coworkers' lost productivity due to their time spent on bringing the new employee "up to speed" or the mistakes made during the indoctrination period.
- putting the person on the payroll, printing business cards, internal and external publicity announcements, establishing e-mail accounts and leasing other equipment such as cell phones, automobiles, pagers.
- a manager's time spent developing trust and building confidence in the new employee's work.

Given the high cost and impact on running a business, a well thought-out program designed to retain employees would easily pay for itself in a very short period of time.

Employee Retention Means a Healthy Bottom Line

Why else is employee retention important? A stable and motivated workforce is the key driver of performance in service businesses. Low employee turnover indicates high employee satisfaction. High employee satisfaction drives customer satisfaction, which in turn drives operating performance. The only "intangible asset" found to predict the future financial performance of a business is its retention rate for key employees.

Employee Satisfaction Cycle

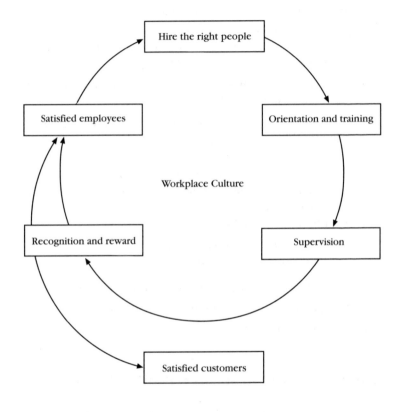

The keys to a stable, motivated workforce are an employee-centered workplace culture and effective employee recruiting and retention practices. Just as you use your brand to raise your profile with consumers, use your brand to lure and keep employees.

What Employees Really Want

How does your organization become employee-centered? By knowing what your employee wants.

Employees want good pay, but they don't always go to the highest bidder. Money isn't everything. And in these increasingly quality-of-life-conscious times, employees are looking beyond financial rewards to other benefits — like flexibility and time with family — in deciding whether to take or keep a job.

Good employees often feel that their employers take them for granted. It takes focus, work and commitment to keep your good employees. The satisfied employee is less likely to search for greener pastures.

There's a whole mix of things that come together to make a company successful at recruiting and retaining employees, but unless there is a corporate culture and a feel to a company that is genuine, the programs don't matter, because they just won't work.

The following will help you lay the foundation for an employee-centered workplace culture. If you additionally use the "best practice" recruiting and retention examples in this book, you will be successful in maintaining low turnover, or reducing turnover where it was previously high. Start with the basics:

- Offer additional training opportunities so employees build new skills to make themselves more attractive for promotion. This not only improves skills, knowledge and performance but also keeps the employees' interest levels high.

- Employees like to know that their opinions count. Give them an opportunity to feel they have some influence. Regular meetings are an excellent way to get employee input, make improvements and address concerns before they become problems. Good employees feel they must have input in the workplace.

- Recognize long-term employees. It gives newcomers a sense of stability within the company. In addition, recognize all good work with financial and non-financial recognition. Good employees expect to be told when they do good work.

- Understand that employees need flexibility. Develop programs that consider them as whole people, not just employees.

- Have fun. No one wants to do boring, drudgery-filled work. A sense of fun and time for recreation adds excitement and keeps attitude high and motivation up.

The successful business of the future will not only attract the best but will create a loyalty to keep the best.

Out of the Mouths of Babes

So how else do you keep good employees around in a job market where the demand for reliable workers exceeds availability? Ask them! Their input will give you the exact information you need to tailor an employee-centered workplace unique to your business culture.

Worker loyalty has decreased in the wake of layoffs, restructuring, mergers, and "rightsizing." All the more reason to pay close attention to what motivates people today.

I created a survey to assess how my prospective employees would rank their priorities. The groups were fairly diverse. I surveyed a fraternity, a group of currently employed caregivers, applicants from a community college career center, active volunteers and Distributive Education Clubs of America (DECA) members. They were asked to rank each of the following seven categories with "1" being their first priority and "7" being their lowest priority. The results were then totaled and divided amongst the participants to give an average score for each category from each group. Consequently, the lower the score, the higher the level of importance.

Each of the seven factors had a description following it. I asked them to rate the following:

Wages — salary, bonuses

Benefits — health insurance, vacation, sick leave, retirement

Environment —job location, overall atmosphere of the location

Reputation — how the company is perceived in the community

People — my friends work here, interview staff is kind, customers and employees seem happy

Flexibility — hours, shifts

Job Duties — I like the job duties required of my position

They gave the following responses, in priority order:

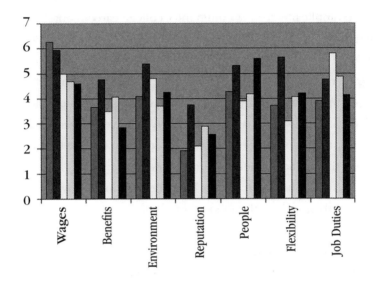

- ■ Fraternity
- ■ Caregiver
- □ College Career Center
- ▨ Volunteer
- ■ DECA

These kinds of surveys give clear clues to organizations that wish to build, or rebuild, loyalty and motivation. For example, although most respondents ranked "reputation" as important, not every group identified it as the top priority. The group of young workers, which includes the fraternity and the DECA Club, ranked wages very low. Remember, this group is looking for job experience and are not as dependent on wages at this point in their life. Consequently, the reputation of the company was extremely important to these young people who are trying to build a résumé.

Of course, what employees want depends very much on the stage each one is at in their career, generational factors, gender, old versus new economy preferences, cultural dynamics and managerial versus implementation roles. This means you must personalize your retention efforts, catering to individual needs and tailoring the employment package. These surveys are an example of how you can assess your own employee pool. By asking and then implementing these wants, you can create a powerful retention tool. The major issue here is that not all line staff's needs are equal. You need to fully understand this issue if you are going to be successful in recruiting, hiring and retaining your staff.

Flavors of Line Staff

Have you ever looked at a business run by a non-profit and been so impressed by their staff that you wonder how they were so lucky to have such sharp employees? Well, it was probably not an accident. More than likely they were focused on getting a different type of employee, the type of employee you won't find in a classified ad. People may say, "Yeah, but they have an unfair advantage. They have a non-profit affiliation that helps them attract people with a social conscience who want to give back." Well, you could have the same type of employee — you just need to think differently.

Far too often as employers, we bemoan the type of problems we have with line staff employees: high turnover, constant complaints, and personal issues. Yes, we lament over the work we put into these employees, but our habits continue to attract this same type. You see, we tend to lump all line staff into the same category when, in fact, all line employees are not created equal.

This chapter will discuss the three different types of line staff employees, their profiles, what motivates them, how to attract them and where to find them. You can then establish retention goals based on the desired percentage of each group over the next year. A better balance of employees between these three groups will allow you to run your operation, reduce costs and cultivate a happier customer. You must recruit differently if you are to attract staff other than those who are career service workers.

But, this won't be easy. You will need to change your way of thinking. Each of the three groups is drawn to service jobs for different reasons and motivation. Even the benefit packages you offer may need to differ from group to group.

Ideally, we would all love to employ a college-educated, 40-year-old homemaker who doesn't need the benefits package and will work a part-time $8-an-hour job to fulfill her mission in life. The problem is this type of employee just doesn't exist in great supply.

Each of the three groups is drawn to service jobs for different reasons and motivation. Even the benefit packages you offer may need to differ from group to group.

As much as we would like to deny it, our current workforce is greatly dependent on the young and relatively unskilled worker. While competing for this type of worker, though, it is imperative to perform one extra step of due diligence.

Due diligence involves breaking the caregiver workforce down into three groups. The first is what I term the *Young Worker*. This marks a rather transient category of staff, typically 16-to-23 years of age, enrolled in college or high school, heavily into activities and their personal lives. The young worker views the job (likely to be their first) as a means for earning discretionary income. Working with the elderly probably seems like a fun departure from the normal retail or fast-food industries to which most of their peers gravitate. Their length of stay in employment is usually less than six months and they are, generally, not the most reliable group.

The second group is comprised of *Career Caregivers.* These people have been involved in nursing care, retirement homes, home health and a variety of other healthcare or service industries. Usually between 22- and 45-years of age, career caregivers tend to be a little older with more work experience than the young worker, and they are often the primary wage earner in the family. The vast majority have children and difficult personal issues going on in their lives outside of work. Most live paycheck to paycheck and will often work other jobs to make more money. Benefits are certainly more important to this group than to the young worker. Career caregivers have chosen this field because it offers them a feeling of self-respect and because it is viewed as more professional than restaurant work. If you are not in the care industry, the equivalent to this group would be career service workers.

Volunteer Worker is somewhat of an oxymoron for the third and final group of workers because they are paid, but it best describes this class of person, who is usually older than 35 years of age and has completed at least a couple years of college. In general, money is not a driver for employment because in many cases someone else is the main provider in the family. Instead, the volunteer worker is driven by the mission of doing good work for a disadvantaged group. They view the job as a way of serving their social conscience. They demand flexibility in their schedule because their life has many components to it, but they are still conscientious and dependable.

Reviewing my own experiences and conversations with caregivers in more than 200 communities, I would estimate that 70 percent of our industry's care staff are career caregivers, 25 percent are young workers, and 5 percent fit the volunteer worker mold. The question is, then, "What does it matter?" It matters a great deal, especially if you believe a more dependable, better-educated and more conscientious staff would benefit your company.

So, the next question becomes "Is it by design or by accident that the make-up of our staff is so disproportionate toward the career caregiver?" I believe it is a blend of both in that it is a "designed accident." We have designed our compensation plans, our benefit plans, our work environments and even our recruitment efforts around the career caregivers. In fact, we have designed a system to get the staff we currently employ.

I'd like to challenge you to a little exercise. Sit down with a list of your staff and divide employees into the three groups: young workers, career caregivers and volunteer workers. Then meet with each group separately. Ask them what motivates them and what brought them to the company. Ask them how they found out about the company. If more than 50 percent say they first learned of the company by reading an ad in the paper, you have a recruitment plan problem. You are not spending enough energy finding the right people.

If staff members say a current employee referred them, this could be good and bad. Referrals by great staff members may, quite possibly, draw similar types of employees. However, if you have staff that needs replacing, then you probably do not want to be recruiting similar types.

You will find these three groups have separate and independent needs from each other. The trick is to get the best mix of these three groups in your work environment. To do this you must be progressive in recruiting the group that best fits your needs.

An entire staff made up of 18-year-old college freshmen may not be a good move. Likewise, hoping that every staff member resembles a 40-year-old homemaker who just happens to be a college graduate is not very likely either.

Career caregivers are some of the best staff that we have. They bring more than philosophy and energy; they bring experience in dealing with real world issues.

So, what is the point? You need to be proactive in how you co-mingle your staff to be representative of all three groups. The night shift needs more than just a warm body. There are ways to have it all, but it means you have to do a couple of things.

As you meet with your staff in separate groups, ask them about their needs and desires. Also ask them the motivation for working in your community. You will find each came to you for a different reason. For example, most often the volunteer worker is not working in your employ because the wages are outstanding. They are working there to get their dose of social redemption. The chart below offers venues and mechanisms to attract each segment. Survey how you recruit and it may answer why you have the employees that you have.

	Career Caregiver	Volunteer Worker	Young Worker
Recruitment Venue	Classified Ads Unemployment Office Friend Staffing Agencies Competition	Churches Synagogues Garden Club Retired Senior Volunteer Program Benevolent Organizations Cultural Arts Magazines	Friends School Counselor DECA Club Future Business Leaders of America School Newspaper
Method of Praise	Public acknowledgement in front of peers	Letter to Pastor Letter to a Benevolent Organization they belong to	Letter to School Counselor Letter to Parents
Primary Reason for Employment	Need money to live	To fulfill social consciousness	Spending Money Work Experience
Important Hard Benefits	Vacation Medical Insurance Bonus Money Any assistance with day-to-day expenses, i.e., daycare, transportation	None	Frequent pay periods
Important Soft Benefits	Work social functions Pleasant physical environment	Public praise Making a difference Flexible Schedule Being treated with respect	Fun Environment Movie Passes Flexible Schedule
Projected Length of Employment	6-12 months	2 years	3-6 months

There are other things you should know about these groups. Let's begin with the young workers.

Young Workers

Young workers are typically flighty; they will probably not work at your organization for more than a few months. There is much you can do to change this pattern. Offer a career opportunity to the young people still going to school and talk with them about the skills they would need to develop in order to advance in your company. Many of our young people are undecided about what they want to do and what classes they should take in college. You have a great opportunity to influence their careers. If they are talented employees, sit down with them and peruse the college catalog together, pointing out what coursework would be helpful if they want to be promoted in the company.

You will also need to be flexible about hours and positions, and you will need to entice the young worker to keep them coming back. I heard of one company that sent out postcards around spring break to young workers who had previously worked for them. The message read "Just wanted you to know that we miss you and your summer job is waiting." What a great tactic! To the employee, this screams loud and clear the company wants him or her back. Now, how much influence do you think this approach has on a 19-year-old mind?

I interviewed 20 young workers to see what qualities they looked for in an employer. In general, these kids held a minimum grade point average of 2.8, all came from middle-class families, and their previous places of employment were health clubs, retail outlets, a bakery, a daycare and various computer-related jobs. Four had worked in senior housing. Ten were male and ten were female. Three of the 20 were ethnically diverse. All but two were either in college or college-bound. I think anyone who employs young people would be happy to have any one of these kids working for them.

I started the questioning by asking how they chose a job. Was it the wages, benefits, the location — what? I was somewhat shocked by the one consistent answer. It seems the main goal for young workers is to have fun on the job. In one form or another, 16 of the kids said the reason they took their job was because it offered a fun environment. Drilling them for more insights on this "fun philosophy," I asked if they would pass up a job that was closer to home and paid more in exchange for one that was fun. The answer was a resounding, "Yes!" Even my own son, Adam, demonstrated the young worker consensus by driving twelve miles each way for a job paying $.25 less per hour than a job he could have had two miles from home.

With this in mind, it is imperative we look at something called the "Mall Syndrome" because this is the environment with which many employers will have to compete. Shopping malls act as social gathering places. Young workers love the idea of working in a mall. It is like getting paid to hang out and meet people — a favorite pastime. Employers housed in these mega-meeting places have a distinct and inherent recruiting advantage over someone who isn't located in a mall.

So what does this mean for those of us who are not in a mall? It means we have to create situations and events that are fun in an effort to please this group of workers. Be prepared to use anything representative of "fun" when recruiting young workers. Let me give you a few ideas. Perhaps you could let them be in charge of organizing an offsite outing for your residents. Or, how about letting them lead an activity on a weekly basis? You could have your young workers teach a class to your residents on something new from their generation. This could be something as funny as having them lead a vernacular class to teach your residents the latest slang version of teenage talk. It doesn't have to be expensive or outlandish — it just has to be fun.

We are living with a generation of children who have been entertained with video games and MTV. Boredom will adversely affect great young workers and they will want to go elsewhere for employment satisfaction.

Half of the responses from these workers indicated they remain in jobs where the responsibilities and duties are enjoyable to them. Three of the respondents said they liked their job because their bosses were friendly and understanding; they felt they could go to the boss with any problems. This fostered a special feeling of loyalty toward the company. Two of the respondents said a boss or coworker helped them solve a major personal problem within the last year. Again, this creates a bond of loyalty and trust thereby enhancing the employer to employee relationship.

After "environment" and "fun," young workers identified "convenience" and "flexibility" as factors they considered important to their personal job selection process. However, their descriptions of convenience and flexibility were far from what I would have imagined. For example, job applications that are short — as opposed to pages and pages in length — are more likely to win favor with this group. This age group is not smitten with filling out forms — the quicker, the easier, the better.

In addition, most of the young workers were amenable to working where they knew someone who could recommend them, as well as set up an interview. They felt this minimized the chances of being rejected. Consequently, most of those interviewed said they relied heavily on word-of-mouth job openings. Ten of the 20 said they had been offered jobs within three days of the last interview for the position. Keep in mind, this is a generation of instant access to information. As the first generation to grow up with the Internet, they have come to expect answers instantaneously. They don't have the patience to wait three weeks for anyone, not even a potential employer, to make up his mind about offering them a job.

All 20 interviewed said flexible schedules were critical. This group has many different activities going on — from school to friends — and they tend to be a very busy group.

The final job attraction for this group is benefits, but not the healthcare or pension plans that would especially interest older workers. The types of benefits that attract this set of workers are what I call soft benefits and include a variety of offerings such as free tanning packages, movie passes, restaurant certificates, discounts at retail chains, help with college tuition or even a health-club membership. With the exception of the tuition reimbursement, all the benefits seem to be activity related and exemplify the types of things that these young workers enjoy in their free time. Although simple in cost and nature, these benefits can pay great dividends thereby adding longevity to your staff. If you choose to incorporate a soft benefits package in order to recruit young workers, make sure you inform job candidates of the details, listing the benefits and how they may obtain them if employed.

Of all the young workers interviewed, not one identified salary or wages as a primary driver in keeping their current job or shifting to another. They all seemed resigned to the fact they would make between $7 and $8 an-hour. Instead, they were much more interested in the already mentioned factors — fun, flexibility and soft benefits.

You must be smart about attracting this group of employees. Not only are they a significant part of the immediate workforce, but you have an opportunity to groom them for the future. Become more sophisticated in your recruitment methods by better understanding their goals in order to retain them. If you have any young workers on your staff, be sure to develop relationships with them so you can better understand this segment of your workforce and respond more effectively to their needs. Young people have constantly changing interests and will be happy to tell you about them if you have created an open and fun environment.

After "environment" and "fun," young workers identified "convenience" and "flexibility" as factors they considered important to their personal job selection process.

We obviously want the best and the brightest this sector has to offer. There are some wonderful young people who bring a great deal of positive energy and enthusiasm to their jobs. Astute companies such as Abercrombie & Fitch have launched major campaigns to attract the best, brightest and most popular young people, adding to the overall success of their operations. An article appearing in the February 8, 2000 edition of *Fortune Magazine* describes CEO Michael Jeffries as a marketing genius for skyrocketing sales at Abercrombie. Just how did he launch the company to revenues of $816 million last year? "Like every youth-clothing maker, Jeffries tells consumers his product will make them cool," the article reads. "But he does much more than that. By hiring the coolest kids and paying them to have fun, he has found a way to package, market and sell popularity."

The study that I conducted with the group of 20 teens was far from scientific. But the point is it may help us understand some of the basic needs of the young worker. It also helps analyze how this group differs from the other segments I have delineated. Hopefully, this will inspire you to develop a more aggressive and strategic recruiting campaign for this segment of your workforce.

Career Caregivers

Now let's turn our attention to the second group of staff, the career caregivers. As I mentioned before, the members of this group typically accept positions within assisted living organizations after working in other healthcare or service industries. They are seeking a long-term position and are often the primary wage earners in their families. Many have children, live paycheck to paycheck, and sometimes work more than one job to make ends meet.

Career caregivers generally fall into the 22- to 45-year-old range and, because of their situations, are more likely to be concerned with the benefits package than the young workers. Oftentimes they select the caregiver career because the position gives them a high degree of self-esteem and personal worth, and in their minds it is a more professional path than working in a restaurant or similar service industry.

I've come to know many career caregivers through personal experience and research. To validate my observations, I selected 20 Áegis care managers that fit my description of career caregiver. Through numerous interviews with these employees, I've come to understand this group better and have been surprised by what I've learned. For example, I expected this group would, in general, be under-educated and lack the drive for a better job. What a pompous fool I was; nothing could have been farther from the truth! In fact, the interviews revealed a lot of truths. The most amazing truth revolved around what motivated these employees to jump out of bed every morning to go to work. Moreover, I was surprised to learn of their career backgrounds and the job offers they had turned down in order to work in our environment.

One of the first questions I asked was why they chose to come to work at Áegis, an assisted living company. Eleven out of the 20 answered that it was their love and desire to work with the elderly. Most of the group described the joy and satisfaction they earned from helping — sometimes even trans- forming — residents' lives on a daily basis. Many commented that it was very gratifying to share in someone else's personal life, perhaps by listening to a memorable story, or seeing a smile on an elderly person's face.

One employee, a 30-year-old male caregiver, explained he had never worked in the long-term care industry previously, but he envisioned the work would be rewarding. He had left a bartending job to join our staff, but noted he was extremely satisfied with his decision to change careers. I wasn't completely convinced a bartender would even want the role of a caregiver, but after getting to know him as well as listening to his fellow employees' praise for him, I'm certain he is doing a wonderful job.

Interviews with the other 19 people revealed they came from all walks of life. There was a postal worker, a beauty-salon owner, a church music director, an optical technician, a warehouse manager, a grocery-store clerk, a collections agent and a florist. Two had been employed in manufacturing, while seven had some healthcare backgrounds including experience in an opthamologist's office, a nursing home, a retirement home, and small board-and-care homes. Three had held positions in various sectors of the service industry.

Oftentimes they select the caregiver career because the position gives them a high degree of self-esteem and personal worth, and in their minds it is a more professional path than working in a restaurant or similar service industry.

One of the most surprising things I learned about this dedicated group was that more than half had left jobs that paid considerably more money! For example, the postal worker had left a $38,000-a-year salary to work with seniors at an average annual wage of less than $17,000. Since joining this industry, 35 percent of the interviewees had even declined job offers from companies that tried to recruit them away from us by paying them higher salaries. Obviously, money isn't the only driver for this group of people. Money is important, of course, because most usually have families to feed and need to make a living. But if money isn't the only motivation to lead someone out the door and into work, what is?

Curious, I asked this group of individuals what motivated them to stay with the company at this lower wage. And, more importantly, what really drew them into work each day? Most reiterated they were gratified by the opportunity to work with elderly residents; they felt their work made a difference in someone's life. Seven of them specified that their positions gave them a sense of value as a person, not just as an employee. A bit confused, I asked if they could explain this to me a little more clearly. I truly enjoyed their answers.

One care manager recalled a specific New Year's Eve night shift she was scheduled to work. As a token of gratitude, her administrator delivered a bouquet of balloons and many thanks for working on the special holiday.

Still others said they appreciated an administrator's open-door policy, allowing them to come in and vent upon occasion. Others noted they greatly enjoyed small parties and barbecues that were hosted in honor of staff. Finally, more than half commented that they had made friends at work and looked forward to socializing with them. The common message was this group of career caregivers wanted to be a part of a great team that really cared about their lives.

Digging a little deeper, I asked them why they decided to leave their last jobs. Many described feeling undervalued as an employee in previous places of employment. One care manager described an instance at a previous employer when she called her boss to say she wouldn't be in that day. Despite the fact that she rarely called in sick, her boss "flew into orbit" demanding she report to her job immediately. She refused and hung up the phone. Within a few hours, she heard someone screaming outside her door. Unbelievably, there was her boss, screaming at her and demanding she come to work. Needless to say, she quit the job and said goodbye to the lunatic.

Satisfied I understood their backgrounds a little better, I decided to ask them some intriguing questions about their current working environment. This helped me tremendously and I highly recommend you do the same. Specifically, I asked what my company could do to improve their working lives.

There were some great insights as well as some startling ones. Of course, I heard the expected "pay us more money," but surprisingly, only six of the 20 blurted out this reply. The most interesting insight is how grateful the staff was that they were even being interviewed by the CEO.

An equal amount said they'd like to see the management fire the under-serving workers. In other words, these care managers took pride in their work and didn't want the environment to be polluted by people who called in sick when they weren't, who didn't genuinely care for the residents, or who were lazy and/or had a bad attitude. They were essentially asking me to partner with them in upholding a quality standard which I fully respect.

Finally, I had half a dozen caregivers thoughtfully mention they would like for everyone to concentrate on offering better care to residents. Most suggestions dealt with improving the activities program or some minor fix to make the residents' lives easier. In sum, I thought this reflected on the unselfish, forever-giving nature of these career caregivers.

I probably could have ended my interview process at this point, but I couldn't resist asking them what they would do if they were the company president, and, of course, what they would consider to be a fair wage for care managers. I received many thoughtful answers. No one made any wisecracks like "pay us $30-an-hour" as you might expect. Instead, 11 of the 20 felt starting wages should be between $8.25 and $8.50 an-hour. The salary could later be bumped up to $9-an-hour if the employee received an exceptional one-year review. (The Federal minimum wage is currently $5.15 per hour. In Washington, where Áegis headquarters is located, the state minimum wage is $6.72).

Six respondents suggested starting staff at $9-an-hour, and then upping it to $10 after one year. Only three commented that starting wages should be $10-an-hour or more. Wages are of course relevant to the local economy. These care managers lived in the San Francisco Bay area, which ranks number one in the highest housing costs in the nation.

All were realistic about what they expected to be paid and had made a conscious decision to accept it even if it meant taking a cut in pay when changing to this new career. Most were comfortable with $9-an-hour plus some medical benefits. They also indicated they would appreciate bonuses based on performance and attendance.

Next, I asked them their views on benefits, especially to determine how benefits could add value to their jobs. Eleven of the 20 suggested a financial bonus be paid quarterly for perfect attendance. This would show that we were placing value on exceptional employees and holding the bar high as an example for others to follow — creating a win-win scenario. Three also added they would like an elective plan that enabled them to customize their own benefits program to make those benefits more valuable and suitable to their personal needs.

I have to say I couldn't have been more pleased with the outcome of my interviews. I learned so much about these employees, and have used this information to better their lives as well as my company. The most obvious conclusion was that career caregivers, like others, choose this line of work for a very specific reason: they love to work with the elderly. They clearly like making a difference in someone's life on a daily basis. Isn't that what we want all of our staff members to feel? These care managers feel that helping these residents lead fuller lives gives them a feeling of self-worth that can't be reflected in a paycheck. Many find their career can even provide more rewards than what they find in their own personal lives.

Although I didn't ask personal questions, many willingly shared stories of their backgrounds and their families. Several emphasized the joy they felt in the beauty of our assisted living homes.

"Sometimes I pretend this is my home," confided one care manager, "and when I come to work I like to think that I'm really coming to my own beautiful home. My own home is not quite as nice."

I was overwhelmed by her compassion as well as the compassion that all 20 care managers had expressed for the residents and the sense of pride they carried around with them just by being a part of this company. Likewise, I felt proud to be in their company. Their stories were full of warmth, fortitude and sincerity. I realized it was an honor to be in communion with them as a team day in and day out. These are the heroes of our industry and I am lucky to know them.

In conclusion, my research with career caregivers revealed that at work, just as in real life, it is often the small things that can mean a lot. Structuring a staff doesn't end with the recruiting and hiring phases if we want to retain these fine people. Payment need not always be in the form of a check. Appreciation can be as simple as a little gesture, a smile or a word of recognition, but the value it holds can far outweigh any dollar amount. Even if you don't operate a senior housing center, the mentality of the career caregiver has application to your service worker.

Create activities in your workplace that encourage your employees to do things that make them feel good about social contribution. If you operate a factory, take a half-day off and work in a homeless shelter with your staff. Contact Habitat for Humanity and build a house as a team. Do something — anything — that tells your staff that as a team, they can work together to make our planet a little better. You will be surprised at the direct correlation such a contribution has at your workplace.

Volunteer Workers

As noted earlier, the volunteer worker is primarily motivated by the mission of giving to others. Oftentimes, these workers have previously held higher-paying jobs, but they are currently seeking a career that offers some degree of social redemption.

In my experience, I have found that most in this group have had some advanced education — usually two years of college — and are around thirty-five years of age or older. Generally speaking, we would be lucky to have even 5 percent of our work force meet the criteria of volunteer worker.

Knowing that volunteer workers are typically excellent employees, particularly for this type of work, I scoured Áegis communities to find qualified individuals to interview. My mission was to see how I could attract more people with the types of backgrounds and experience levels volunteer workers bring to our company. I needed to learn more about their work histories as well as their current and future goals in order to get a bird's-eye view of the big picture. What motivated them to work for us? And, most importantly, what would keep them in our employ?

I asked some executive directors of several assisted living communities to identify people that best resembled volunteer workers. I was lucky to sit down with five individuals, which by no means qualifies this as a scientific survey. Yet I feel I have a greater understanding of this small, but resourceful, group of employees.

"Cashing Out" hypothesizes people will give up high-paying prestigious positions to live a more simple and sedate life, one where old-fashioned values rule and simple pleasures rank supreme. The "Save Our Society" category identifies people who develop strong social consciences and decide they need to be part of the solution to the problems in our society.

The first person I interviewed really blew me away. I was shocked to hear that this employee had been making more than $300,000 a year in a previous job. In fact, all five of the caregivers I interviewed had earned considerably more money than they were currently earning in their new positions. They came from all levels of employment and multiple industries ranging from business owners to techies, medical professionals and salesmen.

What could pull people away from such high-flying, economically gratifying jobs? If you were to ask well-known business futurist, Faith Popcorn who penned the bestseller *Popcorn Report*, she'd explain that volunteer workers fit somewhere in between two of several categorized types of employees/people: "Cashing Out" and "Save Our Society."

"Cashing Out" hypothesizes people will give up high-paying prestigious positions to live a more simple and sedate life, one where old-fashioned values rule and simple pleasures rank supreme. The "Save Our Society" category identifies people who develop strong social consciences and decide they need to be part of the solution to the problems in our society.

Furthermore, Popcorn surmises the rapid and constant communication in our society forces many to become more aware of the world and people. No longer can people remain ignorant of what is going on around them. Hence, educated and informed people begin to feel more responsibility to serve in one way or another.

It was easy for me to see that volunteer workers are at the intersection of these two categories. The first clue was they'd left their high salaries in an effort to make a difference in other people's lives. All of the five interviewed described their new positions as offering them a rewarding experience; they could get a positive and immediate response from residents for whom they were caring. Consequently, they felt they were making a difference.

Two employees explained they'd lived through dramatic life experiences compelling them to seek this type of work. One woman relayed she had been hospitalized with an extreme illness. Touched by the diligent care of the hospital staff, she made a promise to the Lord that if her own health was restored, she would then return the favor by caring for others.

Another employee spoke of the emotional experience she had while caring for her father during his last few days. She came to the revelation that caregiving was her true calling in life, and she made the decision to change careers.

One individual responded that she worked in assisted living not only because it was gratifying to serve residents, but to also have the opportunity to influence young people. She liked the fact that so many young people have chosen to work in this industry, and she saw it as a mentoring opportunity to teach them how to serve others. This was a very important and meaningful life mission for her.

Of course, what I really wanted to know was how I could draw more employees of this caliber to work at our company. How could I go about it? The answer was simple, one person explained, "There are a lot of people out there who are bored with what they are doing. They have had their careers, made money, and now they are looking for a way to give back to their community. Too often, companies are just looking to hire young people." This is shortsighted. Demographics show that employers are facing an increase in older workers and a marked decrease in younger workers over the next ten years. Volunteer workers tend not to retire. Instead, they continue to work either part-time or full-time. They can be a tremendous asset to your organization as well as mentors to your younger staff members.

One interviewee suggested in order to find these types of employees, it might be a good idea to visit meetings of the local garden club, the welcome wagon, or the Junior League. These are places where people are already volunteering their time. It may be resourceful to participate in job fairs in well-established communities where the demographics are representative of this type of worker. The bottom line is this: you can't just run an ad in the paper and expect to get a high-quality worker that fits the description of volunteer worker. Yes, they're out there, but you must be resourceful to find them.

According to my survey group, administrators should spend more time than normal interviewing this category of candidates. "Since this is more of a mission to us than a job," explained one employee, "we want to make sure we are giving our time to the right companies, so we ask more questions about values and purpose of the company than most people might."

In addition, all of our volunteer employees expressed a desire to work in an outstanding, top-notch environment in which the reputation of the company was well-revered. This was extremely important, they said, because they took a great deal of pride in their place of employment, and they wanted to be able to tout where they worked and what they did. This may be why long standing reputable not-for-profits have such a large percentage of volunteer workers.

As I've noted repeatedly we, as employers, are often too self-limiting in our methods of recruiting excellent staff. We hire the people we have always hired in the same manner and through the same routine channels. Their skills and personalities are similar, but their names may change. If we are going to get beyond the crisis that now exists in finding quality staff, we have to throw away our current paradigm for recruiting.

The volunteer worker can provide a workforce that is reliable, educated, mature and compassionate about what they do. What more could an employer want? This small sect of workers will not solve the total evolving staff crisis, but these people can supplement and enhance our workforce. Moreover, the influence these workers may have on other staff members could be immeasurable. Don't overlook the rewards gained by seeking out these very special employees.

Retention Nuggets

CHAPTER 3

Loyalty Links

Loyalty Links may seem odd phraseology, but it's likely you will embrace the concept once you see the powerful effect it can have on your operation. A Loyalty Link is an act by an employer that goes beyond the typical employer/employee relationship interaction that helps create a bond of trust.

The concept is often associated with smaller company, old-school thinking. You have heard the stories before where an employer loans money for an employee's child's surgery or the company signs for a personal loan. These actions create an environment in which the employee views his employer as a personal resource — someone who has a vested interest in his or her welfare. These acts of loyalty to the employee create a link that bonds employer and employee. Consequently, employees are less likely to leave for an extra $.25 offered by your competitor.

Big companies usually frown on actions like these. The reasons are many: "We cannot do that or we will have to do that for everyone." Or, "There is too much liability for the company." And, even another, "Our shareholders wouldn't find that accretive to the company's bottom line."

In response to all these reasons (which are really only lame excuses), I would say "Poppycock." Again, our epidemic of staff loss is costing us millions of dollars annually in over-time, loss of revenue and training expenses. We have no choice but to go the extra mile for our staff because the staggering truth is the average $8.00/hour employee costs $50,000 to replace. Employee turnover is very costly to an organization and, ultimately, takes its toll on organizational performance, productivity, and profit.

Employee loyalty has greatly diminished since the 1960s. In the past, employees believed when a company hired them that they would be with that company until they retired. Starting in the 1980s as companies sought to increase profits, workers' perceptions of lifetime employment were shattered by corporate downsizing, company relocations to other states or countries, and static wages.

The perception of job security today has changed. Employees now enter employment relationships with an inherent mistrust. This mentality exists until an employer does something to prove the theory incorrect. That is why looking for Loyalty Links and creating a caring culture for employees is extremely valuable. I am not suggesting you pretend to care about your staff as a way to send a message to the masses. Instead, I am saying that it is imperative to your operations that you do, indeed, care for your employees. Using Loyalty Links as a conscious strategy is vital.

As proof, throughout this book, I include examples of things that have worked within my company, but I also share ideas by others that I have discovered in my research. The point of these examples is not to have you emulate them, but rather to realize that when these situations occur you should recognize them as an opportunity to foster loyalty. Some of the items are strategic in nature and can be done on an ongoing basis; others are isolated incidents that were spur of the moment.

Regardless, they all had the same effect. They left the employee feeling as though they were more than a name on a timecard. They were made to feel as though they were cared for as a person.

One of the things I have always wanted for the staff of Áegis is for people to feel as though we are a family. By that, I mean our culture should be sensitive to the employee's total world, not just their work world. The family includes the employees, but also extends to the employees' families.

When we started the company, I wanted to acknowledge the often-grueling decisions that entire families can go through when one family member joins a new company. Áegis was a new company, and most of the staff we wanted to recruit hailed from big established companies. I knew the recruits would have to give up many things including higher wages and better benefits as well as the stability of their job and position.

As a result of the transition, the family as a whole is subjected to some trauma. What if the company goes broke? What if business doesn't grow like the company plans? What if the employee doesn't live up to the new expectations? In addition, sometimes family plans have to be put on hold while the new employee tests the waters. All these concerns cause a great deal of anxiety for the new employees and their families.

So, what can you do about this as an employer? Simply start by acknowledging it.

I started writing letters to all new corporate and field managers' families. It worked well when I started the company, so I have continued this practice. I find out who plays the central support role for this person and then write a letter to that person. I have written to spouses, boyfriends, girlfriends and partners. I have even written to the employee's parents. This may not seem like an amazing idea, but the response has been incredible.

One of my staff member's wives called me in tears one day and said, "My husband has worked for bigger and more famous companies, but none that have ever come close to being so thoughtful. Our decision to join your company was a difficult one, filled with some uncertainty. After receiving the letter, I know we made the right choice. By the way, I framed the letter and have it in my office to show everyone how proud I am to have my husband work for a company like Áegis." A five-minute effort yielded tremendous results. Families marvel at receiving a letter from a busy CEO simply thanking them for choosing to trust the company. This kind of effort depicts the culture of the company.

It is more important that your efforts are sincere rather than expensive. A few years ago a manager of mine called to reminisce about us working together. He asked, "Do you know what memory I value the most from when I worked with you?" I racked my brain to think of some great business challenge that we conquered together, but nothing rushed to the forefront. So I responded, "No, what do you value most?" "It was when you interrupted your family vacation to console me after discovering my father died unexpectedly. That gesture meant so very much to me as a person."

We tend to forget that our employees are human beings with the same problems and issues that our own families have. I've heard wonderful stories about companies that acknowledge and understand this. While one employee was battling a bout with cancer, her manager made sure food was delivered to the house on a regular basis. Staff members donated vacation time to another employee who needed to care for her ailing parents. A costly prescription drug was underwritten for another employee's child. One of the greatest challenges facing company leaders today is to understand and accommodate their employees' real-life issues. That's why at the brokerage house, Edward Jones, managers are encouraged to "do what's right and human."

Loyalty Links are more easily defined by effort. A manager taking time out of his or her hectic day just to acknowledge an employee means so much to that employee. You don't need to break the bank on items — just break the brain on being creative. People have an inherent need to be valued as people. Your staff will present you with daily opportunities for Loyalty Links. Do not let them slip by under the guise of violating corporate policy. Take advantage of building your employer/employee relationships, and watch how it can affect your staff's morale.

Designing Environments

How much time, as managers, do we really take to design environments that promote the success of our staff? When you think about a staff break room, does the image of a cramped, paint-peeling, ancient magazine-ridden backroom come to mind? How do we tell our staff that we value them yet provide only a folding chair in a closet for them to escape for a break? Good employees expect their employer to be making constant improvements so the workplace is not only safe, but pleasant.

This is a mistake I have made at Áegis. It really did not cross my mind that break rooms were important. But I learned these rooms should be a welcoming oasis in the middle of an often traumatic work environment. We have now started to look at how the room could be used, what amenities the staff would like and where the room should be located in the building. Putting a lot of thought into your break rooms will leave your staff appreciative of the sensitivity you have for them.

There are some simple rules to follow when planning a comfortable break room. Poll your staff to see how the room is used. How many people will be using this area at one time? Don't have a break room that seats only three people if six people will be on break at once.

Design the area so people will actually want to use it. Do people go there to relax and have some quiet time to read or just close their eyes for a few minutes? If so, think about providing magazines, a drinking fountain, a comfy massage chair, fluffy pillows and even a dimmer on the lights. Conversely, if the area is more of a socializing spot for the majority, you may want to have music and possibly video games.

If the spot is also used for snacks and meals, you should probably provide a refrigerator, microwave, coffee pot and vending machines. Drinks and snacks for your night staff might be greatly appreciated if they have no other place to get nourishment.

I visited the break room at a Four Seasons Hotel. This room was filled with items that encouraged the staff to look their best. The hotel provided items for primping, much like you would find in a nice restaurant washroom. The hotel even had a stickpin polishing cloth for the doorman. This level of detail conveyed the message that there is a superior expectation and a laser focus on the details. The break room functioned as a living environment for the company's culture.

Some managers may worry that if the break room is too attractive, people will spend all their time in there. This is old-school thinking. Realize the work you have people doing is difficult and, in order for them to be productive, they need some place to recharge their batteries. Sit down with your staff and ask them what they would like to have in their break room. I think you will be surprised at the simple and inexpensive items they request. The net value of caring for your staff and showing your appreciation by having a great break room will far outweigh the risk associated with people who might abuse it.

The "Treat Philosophy"

In May 2000, I was acting out one of my childhood fantasies by driving CART race cars at Sears Point in Sonoma, California. Taking a break from the track, I met a gentleman who owned a small chain of screw and fastener stores. He talked about his company with great pride, particularly noting that he had little turnover among his managers. I informed him I was writing this book and asked him if he might share some of his expertise. He told me that he subscribed to the "Treat Philosophy" of retention.

This businessman explained that for a number of years he had tried to motivate people by giving them bonuses or large salary increases, but he concluded that this didn't do much to retain long-term individuals. So, a few years ago, he started to give people special treats they would never buy for themselves, but would love to have. In fact, that was precisely the reason he was there the day I met him. He had brought one of his long time managers to the racing school, decked him out in racing gear and given him first-class treatment for four days.

"When I give my employees a cash bonus, it usually goes to something practical like buying furniture or paying off a credit card," he said. "But when I do something like this, it is a memory that lasts forever."

The gentleman continued to explain how the Treat Philosophy works as leverage in his business. "People will have pictures posted all over their office, and they'll be telling other employees that the company paid for this experience. Then you start a domino effect, because people will ask how they can receive the same treatment."

It seems the Treat Philosophy can have a more lasting effect on employees than a basic bonus check because, when you think about it, no one is going to have a picture of their bonus check posted in their office. These experiences not only last a lifetime, but also create goodwill in the work environment for years to come. I once sent one of my Áegis managers on a trip for a job well done. This manager still has pictures of the trip on his office wall. When other employees come in and ask about the trip, it recreates the memories all over again.

This store owner had truly mastered the motivation of his employees and he knew how to keep them happy. He said a critical piece of the equation was finding the "treats" employees like, which means spending time getting to know your people. For some, the bonus of a lifetime might be driving CART race cars while others might like a weekend getaway, a day at a spa or a weekend driving around in a rented Jaguar. There are many ways to make the Treat Philosophy work in your favor. Get to know your people and be creative when treating them to the memory of a lifetime.

POW Retention Policy

All right, the phraseology may be a little overkill but let me make my point. I am referring to all those companies who have agreements presumably preventing an employee from ever working for a competitor the rest of their natural born life.

Don't get me wrong. I think employment contracts have their place in this world. You don't want your software engineer at Microsoft to go and work for Sun Microsystems. You don't want your nuclear engineer to go from the state department to the Russian KGB. You don't want your lead design engineer to go from Ford to General Motors. In those examples, we are talking about protecting millions — maybe billions — of dollars for the company. Some top-secret information could have a detrimental effect on a company and may even put a company out of business if it were leaked. But let's do a reality check here. We are talking about a service industry that has very few trade secrets. Are we afraid that someone is going to discover how we make meatloaf or that our rent roll is the key to our success?

I know the reason employers try to enforce employment contracts. It's so that another company does not steal your good people. Let's think about that reason for a millisecond. We are not talking about raiding corporate headquarters with machine guns and putting hoods over people's heads and carrying them off to tell us the secret formula of the Atom Bomb. That would constitute stealing your employees. The simple reality is that someone wants one of your great employees.

They make your employee a better offer and lure them away. No stealing, kidnapping or forced abduction here. Now you're mad because you have trained and invested in someone only to lose him or her to your competition. The end result is a double whammy of negative consequences.

Employment contracts have a negative connotation to people. People interpret them as a very cold way to control staff. These contracts essentially state "You are my property because I gave you a job and training. Now you need to spend the rest of your life indebted to me." It doesn't matter if someone is prepared to offer the employee double their salary or if the responsibilities at the new job would be a once in a lifetime opportunity for the employee. If those of you who make use of employee contracts are saying to yourself, "Well, if it was really that big of deal I would release them from the contract," be careful. You now create a precedent for the entire company. You cannot randomly select which employment contract you can or cannot honor.

So, what do you do instead of having employment contracts? Know how to keep employees happy, know what people earn in the job market for their positions, know what types of benefits are offered, and know what motivates your employees. Moreover — the big one — tell them how much you appreciate them on a constant and daily basis. Feed their soul. Of the many staff that I have interviewed, over 90 percent said they had been offered a job in the past year for more money, but they had turned it down because they liked the way in which they were currently treated. None said they turned it down because they were bound by an employment contract.

If your employee gets an offer, celebrate their departure. Make a big deal out of how proud you are this person has such a great opportunity. Let them know that you feel very privileged to have been a part of their career growth and that the door is always open if they wish to come back. Nevertheless, don't trap your employees. You will find the staff will harbor tremendous resentment toward the corporate office. Unhappy employees are not good employees.

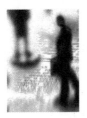

Organization Planning

CHAPTER 4

Organization Planning for Hiring and Retaining Goals

The key, of course, to retaining exceptional employees is to hire right. At least half of the personnel problems I see my colleagues struggle with are caused by poor hiring policies.

Recruiting and retaining key staff is similar to relationship selling. Relationship selling is a series of marketing steps successful sales people follow in order to obtain solutions. The same steps are necessary in hiring. You work at finding the best potential employees and offer them a product or solution for their specific needs. This book shows you how to effectively source candidates, how to write ads that will improve the quality and quantity of the responses you receive, how to select the right candidates to invite in for interviews, and then how to retain these employees. With these steps, you make fewer hiring mistakes, attract a stronger team, and improve your operational performance.

First, you need organization planning. This is an up-front human resource and organizational needs assessment that helps you determine your hiring and retention goals and measures. The process is a yearly projection with quarterly reviews.

Organization planning will help you determine the following:

- Who you need
- When you need them
- The flow of applicants
- The necessary reallocation of resources
- The sourcing mix

Organization planning also addresses these other issues:

- Structuring the organization
- Determining what training, mentoring and coaching are needed
- Assessing accountability roles
- Creating communication channels
- Matching skills

A staff vacancy can arise from various events such as voluntary or involuntary separations, increased workloads, promotions, increased census or restructuring of a department. Therefore, the first step in the recruitment process should be to evaluate if there is a need to hire.

In the case of an open position resulting from a separation, consider whether the job responsibilities can be absorbed by other positions or eliminated all together. Perhaps the position can be changed to a part-time or temporary status. If you plan to eliminate a position, your needs assessment and wide-range sourcing strategy should take this into account. More specifically, you should develop a succession or "back-fill" strategy before an incumbent is separated from your organization.

Here is a list of questions to ask to determine your human resource needs:

- What is my turnover rate?
- How much attrition do I anticipate?
- Why am I experiencing turnover?
- Where am I experiencing turnover?
- What are my census projections?
- How do my census projections correlate with my human resource projections?
- What am I doing to capture the knowledge of critical staff members?

To determine your organization needs, ask the following questions:

- Will I need to change my organizational structure to accommodate these new staff members?
- Will I need to add training, coaching and mentoring?
- Will I need to change who reports to whom?
- Is there an internal candidate for this position?
- Will the current reward system still be effective?
- What are my direct and indirect competitors doing to attract qualified candidates?
- Am I going to need to increase wages to attract qualified candidates? If so, how will this impact internal equity with existing staff members?
- What skill levels do I need?
- Will cultural diversity be impacted?
- Are current communication methods still going to be effective?
- Is the current performance management system still going to be effective?

There are worksheets in the Appendix to assist you in your own planning process. At the end of each quarter, you should evaluate the success of your recruiting strategy by explaining any variances and your plans to address them.

Stand by your Brand

Next, you must brand your organization so you can successfully market it to potential employees. Write a description of what makes your business the business of choice. Your organization's story is your "great place to work" brand.

Stand by your brand — it's the promise that you keep. It's your guarantee. Your brand is what your employees and customers see as the ongoing worth of a relationship with your business. All actions and messages are based on the value the organization brings to its level of business.

The brand is where what the customer and employee values intersects with the company strengths. To get there, ask yourself the following: Who are we? Where did we come from? Where are we going? What are we doing here?

What makes our story meaningful? Does it capture the heart of our organization in a way that evokes strong emotions? Does it reflect company values? Does it capture our vision?

Your story needs to be compelling, compact and realistic. Your story should have a condensed version that takes no longer than 30 to 45 seconds to relay. You must make sure your story is not selling the candidate a bill of goods or baiting people into the organization. A compelling realistic story will help candidates self-select so you are sure to have a good organizational match.

Steps for Sourcing

CHAPTER 5

After completing your organization planning, there are various ways to find your best-qualified candidates. Problems arise when only one path is chosen. Finding good candidates can be tricky. It requires ingenuity and strategic planning. Analyze the position criteria before choosing the most appropriate tactics.

Let's assume you're on the right track in the initial stages of hunting for the perfect employee. You have staked out the best haunts for prospective staff and you're writing a stimulating ad, targeting the right newspapers and periodicals. Now what? Should you just sit back and rely on the traditional hiring model that will prove frustrating at best — if not futile? Not even for a second!

Be vigilant in removing employment barriers. The following simple tips can be very effective tools for helping you pre-qualify prospective employees.

The Advertisement

I am not a big advocate of using classified ads for finding the right employee, but they have their time and place. In addition, they can be a viable venue to include in your sourcing mix. When you do use classified ads, make sure you're getting the biggest bang for your buck.

There are many schools of thought behind writing a "Help Wanted" ad. Some say it is best to write a "grabber" and pull people in with something that captures their attention. Others advise to keep it short and sweet and to the point. Still others like to create ads that are filled with mystery and intrigue, not really telling the job seeker anything about the position that is open.

My preference is to be up-front, informative and honest. But there must also be something to attract the candidate's interest. Mention, for example, a casual atmosphere or bonus potential. These features will stand out to potential candidates. In addition, give the candidate some insight as to the culture of the business, especially if this is a positive selling point.

An ad in the Sunday edition of a major metropolitan newspaper can run upwards of $2,000 if it is very descriptive and runs several inches. Plus, you are still in the middle of hundreds of other competing ads.

Focus the ad copy on what the person needs to do and is expected to accomplish. Give them a vision of how they will grow and develop the first year. Don't pack the ad with lists of required skills, academics and duties. Experience is a poor predictor of on-the-job success, so keep it to a minimum in the copy. Focus on attracting the best by painting a compelling future.

Use the boiler plate ad in the Appendix to create your own ad.

Here are some examples:

HOT SHOT HOUSEKEEPER

Begin your new life with us. Only the best will do! If you take pride in your work, love people, and want to be a member of a great assisted living community, come by and apply in person. You'll get good benefits, a good salary and more. You'll be the expert in standards of cleanliness and make a difference in our residents' lives. Please come by if this makes sense to you and be prepared to tell us why.

Áegis of Anytown
Address
Phone Number
We value diversity in our workforce.

MEDICAL TRANSCRIPTIONISTS

We asked our Medical Transcription Team what they liked best about working for us and they said:

* Excellent Salary/Benefits   * Casual Dress
* Retirement Plan   * Flexible Hours
* Advancement Opportunities   * Tuition Reimbursement
* Flexible/Supportive Supervisors   * Training Programs
                 * Spacious Relaxed Atmosphere

Candidates will have two years recent acute hospital transcription experience; record of good attendance/dependability; knowledge of medical terminology, anatomy and physiology; and must be able to work independently. Apply online referencing job #2001 or visit our Employment Office at

Address
Phone Number
Individuals who are bilingual or have multicultural or
diverse patient population experience are encouraged to apply.

MANAGER – SMALL BUSINESS DEVELOPMENT

JOBS WITH PURPOSE – CAREERS WITH VISION

Become part of a greater mission by supporting our efforts to bring together community resources and achieve a vision of a vital economy with healthy neighborhoods and quality jobs for all citizens.

In this position, you'll be the small business advocate, and oversee small business activities including policy development, program development and implementation. Your primary responsibilities include small business retention, oversight of small business programs and small business development city-wide. Additional responsibilities include budget, program objectives and work plans, and management of staff.

Successful candidate will have an MBA or MA in business or related field, specializing in business management, finance or economics, and six years' supervisory and/or a progressively responsible position. Must possess strong organization and team-building skills, effective writing, public speaking and interpersonal skills. Knowledge of problem-solving techniques, budgeting processes, progressive general management skills, and business management is essential. Limited Term 2 Years.

Pick up an application packet at:
Address
Phone Number

Fish in the Right Pond

To effectively recruit employees, target the areas in which prospects live and the periodicals they read. It is no different than marketing a business in which you match your customers' demographics with the appropriate advertising vehicles.

I once posted an ad in a major regional newspaper for an Áegis property in need of care staff. The ad cost a bundle yet solicited little response. So, I turned to the local ad newspaper, similar to ones you've probably seen in your own community such as *The Money Saver, The Nickels Worth, The Penny Saver,* etc. A strange venue for employment, you may think, but the responses started rolling in. One ad drew thirty-five applicants. The ad cost one-tenth of the one in the larger newspaper, but the results were ten-fold.

Simply put, you need to understand your audience. Most people who make $8 to $10 an-hour don't subscribe to *The Los Angeles Times* or *The Chicago Tribune.* Moreover, they don't look for jobs there. They tend to stick to the communities and media venues close by. These little papers are convenient, free and sometimes even delivered to the doorstep of your potential employee. Know where your dollars are going to get the biggest bang. Start by asking your current employees what they read and take it from there.

One of the most creative ideas I've heard comes from Jim Treadway, a previous president of Westin North America. He suggests drawing a ten-mile ring around your business and then determining where the low-income or subsidized housing communities are located. Ascertain the predominant ethnic population and write your ad in their language. In the ad, offer a unique "grabber" such as English as a second language (ESL) classes at no charge. If certain positions don't require employees be fluent in English, be sure it is prominently noted. Place these ads on bulletin boards throughout the housing community. Treadway claims to have hired several people a year through this very inexpensive resource.

You don't always have to spend major dollars to attract great employees. Start with the things that cost little or nothing. About twelve years ago, I hired a number of employees that responded to ads posted in laundromats around the city. While waiting for their laundry to dry, they would read the message board with information about my retirement home. It cost me practically nothing and supplied me with good, honest workers. Other possible outlets include bus stop benches, church bulletins and college newspapers — all of which are free or inexpensive vehicles for your message.

The bottom line is that you must think like the employees you are trying to hire. Think about their lifestyle, where they live, where they shop, how they travel and where they spend their time. You will not find a universal medium for all markets. It will be incumbent upon you to find out what works and what doesn't. But make your mistakes on the ads that cost $50 a run as opposed to those costing $2,000.

Display Ads

Instead of small classified ads, you can buy a larger block of space on the classified pages and run an attractive display ad. Because your ad must compete with many other display ads, it must be well-designed and distinctive. These ads are often very expensive, so it's advantageous to target several positions at once with one ad.

In addition, there is a lot more to a newspaper than the classifieds. Taking into account the audience for which you are aiming, consider other sections of the paper such as the Business, Sports or Entertainment pages.

Blind Ads

Blind ads, which do not identify the company, are used by some businesses to cut costs and to avoid having to deal with unqualified applicants. But blind ads don't always allow you an opportunity to promote your brand, which in turn helps applicants self-select — or self-disqualify — themselves.

There are other problems with blind ads. For example, current staff members may answer the ad or find out they were not considered for a promotion.

Although it is additional work, you should maintain your image and goodwill in the community by answering all applications with a simple form letter, postcard or electronic auto response.

Take This Job and Post It

Another recruitment tool to investigate is the Internet. More and more people are using the Web to look for employment. Although not every household in America has a computer, the ability to access a computer is becoming very easy. Just as with voicemail, you can easily post job announcements on your Web page including locations, job descriptions and benefits. Web pages can provide more visually graphic information about your company including pictures of the buildings, employees interacting with clients, etc. It also allows people to print the information so they may reference a hard copy.

Some companies have even gone to the extent of allowing candidates to apply for jobs over the Internet. Job applications can be filled out directly on the Web site and e-mailed to the appropriate person.

Make sure your human resources person is prepared to deal with large volumes of unsolicited résumés in this day of the Internet. Résumé spamming, which easily allows candidates to send their résumés to multitudes of online job boards like www.monster.com and www.gojobs.com as well as your Web site, can be an enormous source of résumés.

Aside from having an applicant tracking system with a sophisticated search engine, an effective way to find qualified candidates is through screening and assessment tools. There are many available online that can be integrated into your Web site or third-party assessment site.

Remember that time is of the essence when you recruit off the Internet. If the candidate has posted his or her résumé on the Web, she/he is fair game for hundreds of other potential employers. Although this is becoming common for management-type positions, I believe line staffers are more inclined to stop by the office and pick up an application. Don't overestimate the power of the Internet nor underestimate the power of the other tools discussed. Use what is most appropriate for the positions you want to fill.

You, as an employer, really need to assess what the barriers are in your local community and decide how you are going to remove them. The major mistake employers make is to not give enough thought to possible obstacles. Potentially good employees may be deterred from applying for a job because of an easily removed obstacle. For example, someone depending on public transportation may not know the local bus stops one block from your building. Sitting down with your current staff to ask what some of the obstacles were for them is likely your best source of information. Take advantage of it.

Information Please — Voicemail

Set up a voicemail account and publish the phone number in your ads. The voicemail prompts will guide the candidate to the job that is of most interest and supply him or her with the details of the process.

The voicemail should begin with a general message stating a philosophical overview of the company. Here's an example:

"You have reached Bonanza Assisted Living Company's employment line. Bonanza Assisted Living is committed to exceptional customer service for frail, elderly seniors throughout the Northeast. We operate 24 assisted living communities serving more than 3,000 residents. Bonanza has been in business for 26 years and has been a recipient of the 'John Simmons Best Employer Award' for the last six years."

The caller then listens to voicemail prompts with directions to push specific numbers which correspond to job positions. For example, the candidate may be instructed to push the number "1" for information on care manager positions. The voicemail would then play a message such as the following: "We are presently looking for care managers at our location in

Hartford, Connecticut. The position of care manager involves dealing with frail, elderly people on a daily basis.

"Duties include bathing residents, assisting in the changing of residents who are incontinent of bladder and bowel, assisting in dressing residents and other duties that may be necessary when dealing with a frail population. The starting wage is $8.50 an-hour with a performance raise in 90 days. Exceptional staff may be entitled to as much as $.75 an-hour more. You may also be entitled to our instant bonus program that rewards staff members for going above and beyond the call of duty. Our best workers made an additional $500 last year.

"Hartford's benefits package includes medical and vision to all employees working a minimum of 20 hours. Scheduling is flexible.

"Hartford Assisted Living is conveniently located two blocks from the rapid transit system that serves 26 cities throughout the region. We also offer Rapid Transit discounts throughout our company. Please call Nancy Smith at (800) 787-0000 for more information about the position."

This voicemail message has just saved you time and money. First, it qualifies people according to pay scale. The voicemail also outlines other compensation, including benefits. Employees are competitive shoppers these days. It is important to state what the best performers could possibly earn. Although line staff may be less than 10 percent of your workforce, most people aspire to be the best worker. They are looking for the best deal they can get. Realize that this voicemail is a recruiting effort; give it your best shot to persuade the candidate to go to the next step.

Secondly, the voicemail message clarifies the real-life duties of working as a care manager. Too often we deliver a cushy description of a job that really involves more nitty-gritty work. This is a primary culprit for high staff turnover. I have heard management staff try to recruit employees by telling them how fulfilling their job will be when reminiscing with the elderly over the previous eighty years of their lives. Later, when the care manager is struggling to get a 200-pound resident out of bed in the morning, the recruitment pitch will be recalled in anger and the employee will feel misled. While it is true that staff may have some engaging times with residents, it is probably safer to give potential employees glimpses of worst-case scenarios so they are better prepared for the job should they be hired.

Always make sure the voicemail recording gives the candidate a telephone number and preferably a person's name with whom to follow up. People are more inclined to take things to the next step if they can call someone for quick answers to questions. Once again, these telephone calls are recruiting opportunities. Make sure your staff appreciates this and avoids viewing them as interruptions in their day. The interaction with staff could make or break the candidate's decision to join your company.

Here's another idea: if you are in the pre-opening stage of business or are only open during normal operating business hours, install a real estate box near the front door and use it as a "Help Wanted" application box. Signage on the box should indicate it contains job postings and applications. Make sure to keep the box filled with applications, lists of positions and job descriptions. People can then stop by any time to obtain employment information and an application. It is especially suitable for those who can't break away during typical business hours. Make sure to let people know on your voicemail that this arrangement is available. Since the people you really want to hire probably already have jobs, provide an easier process for them to learn about openings within your company. The "Help Wanted" box should include a mail slot through which completed applications can be dropped. You will be surprised at how many more applications you will receive.

Always in the Business of Recruiting

About 12 years ago, while I was administrator of an assisted living building in Kennewick, Washington, I ran into a neighbor of mine at the grocery store. As we chatted, she told me she had heard great things about my organization and had always wanted to work there. Knowing it was such a great place to work, though, she just assumed there was rarely any turnover. I was dazed.

First of all, I had thought that I had done everything possible to put the word out that we were hiring. Secondly, I did not think to tell my own circle of friends that I was looking for people. Lastly, I realized I needed to stop being so conventional by relying so heavily on newspapers and the unemployment office.

I did several things after that meeting with my neighbor. I immediately hired her. Then, I put a large reader board on our sidewalk advertising our need for employees. I realized not everyone read the local newspaper as I did.

Going where the people are has turned the world into a job fair for me. I constantly hand out business cards telling people I'm always hiring and encouraging them to call me personally if they are looking for a job. I do this with my neighbors, my church group, the Chamber of Commerce, the parents of my kid's Little League — absolutely everyone. When I go into a restaurant and see a great worker, I give them my card and ask them to call me if they are ever looking for a job change.

Some people have frowned on this practice saying that it means you are continually trying to recruit someone else's staff. My response is that everyone comes from some previous job. You cannot kidnap staff; they will come by their own free will. The only difference is that you have the opportunity to conduct a working interview, of sorts, with that staff member. By seeing them in action with customers, whether it was pouring coffee, checking a guest in or making a bed, you have a working interview. This practice has yielded some of my best employees.

A senior manager recently asked me if an overload of employment advertising would send a negative message to the customer, specifically that our business was unstable or could not keep good staff. Although that certainly is possible, I think the alternative is a greater risk. The alternative is that you do not have good staff or maybe no staff at all. The general public knows the job market is tight. In fact, many of our customers are experiencing the same dilemma in their own businesses. The fact that unemployment is low is not a well-kept secret. Should a customer inquire, the response should be a simple "We are always looking for great staff."

Follow Your Staff

Follow your staff when they leave. I don't mean jump in your car and tail them; I mean keep current on the exceptional people who leave your employ for one reason or another. Maybe you already do this in an informal manner. What I am suggesting is a formal process whereby you chart where your good former employees have gone and for what reason. Then, you assign someone to call them every other month to see how their current job is going and if they are happy. If not, perhaps they'll consider returning to your company.

Should a customer inquire, the response should be a simple "We are always looking for great staff."

If you are hesitant about re-hiring people who have departed, think about it in these terms: you had a great employee who was a proven product to you. You know all their idiosyncrasies and deficits; you know their strengths. Doesn't it make better sense to re-hire and know what you're getting (not to mention the fact you don't have to re-train these people) than to constantly run ads in the paper and take a chance on a person known only by a name, résumé and a two-hour interview?

A former employee is reluctant to call a previous employer even if their current job isn't working out. When I have interviewed line staff in the past, I've asked them about their best job experience. After they told me with great enthusiasm what it was, I asked why they never went back to that employer to ask for a job. Most said they felt embarrassed or awkward asking to be re-hired by a former employer. Why? Almost all answered they had informed their employer they were going on to something more fulfilling with more money or more responsibility. When they gave notice, they made it sound like the job offer was too good to pass up. So when the job didn't work out, they couldn't go back and say, "Well, I was fooled. My job wasn't as great as I thought it was going to be. Can I have my old job back?"

My advice to employers is "take heed." We know employees are probably not going to return unless they are asked. So when a prime employee leaves, my suggestion is to call them and call them and call them. Why? When I asked the interview candidates if they would have returned if their old bosses had called to tell them they were missed and asked to return, all replied "yes!"

When people feel wanted and needed, it gives them immense job satisfaction. Call your former good employees. Tell them how much you miss them, the residents miss them, the customers miss them — but call them. This is one of those things that fall through the cracks. Everyone says, "Yes, that is a great idea." But then, no one does it.

So, here is what you need to do to be successful. Each month, designate a list of callback employees. Give someone in your office the responsibility of generating this list each month. Another employee should be assigned the responsibility of doing the callbacks. Former employees should be called every couple of months because situations change frequently, and you want to call when the person is contemplating to leave. Also on a monthly basis, meet with the team making the callbacks and discuss each former employee's status. Make sure your team is asking the right questions to determine if the former employee is happy in their current position, what keeps them in the position, and what would it take for your company to get them back.

Perhaps they want to make $.50 more an-hour or they only want to work swing shifts. If this is the case, you may want to make concessions. As a matter of practicality, though, you may not want the person who calls the former employee to be negotiating a return package. Instead, the former employee should receive a follow-up call from the appropriate manager to discuss a re-hire. This gives you or the decision-making manager some time to think about the requests, and how they may impact the rest of the employees if you concede to them. This process may seem very time-consuming, but it really takes no more than a couple of hours per month once you've mastered it. Moreover, re-hiring even two or three staff members a year could save you thousands of dollars per year in training and recruiting efforts.

One last thing to consider is that the person's employer may accuse you of trying to steal his or her employee. You can simply remind the employer where the employee came from — your company. If the former employee asks you to stop calling, though, you should honor the request. Remind the former employee that you hold them in high regard and they are always welcome to call you to discuss employment.

Employee Referrals or Keeping It All in the Family

Many companies like Alaska Airlines have found employee referral programs are one of the most cost-effective recruiting methods available to find qualified candidates. In today's labor market, what better way is there to find talent as well as retain your current employees than by rewarding referrals?

Furthermore, a 2001 survey by the Society for Human Resource Management and Referral Networks of 586 human resource professionals indicated 80 percent felt employee referral programs were more cost-effective than job search firms. Almost 70 percent said that employee referral programs were more cost-effective than other recruiting practices. In addition, 36 percent said employee referral programs were effective or extremely effective.

In today's labor market, what better way is there to find talent as well as retain your current employees than by rewarding referrals?

Money and gift certificates are among the incentives offered in employee referral programs. And, in most cases, the amount of the award is predetermined and distributed after a required tenure period of the new hire.

In my own organization, anyone who refers a candidate for a position is entered into a monthly drawing for a prize which can range from movie tickets to a paid day off. The staff member who recommends the candidate who successfully secures the position receives a referral bonus, which is paid in two installments. The first installment is paid to the referring employee after the new staff member's 30-day anniversary; the second installment is paid on the event of the 90-day anniversary. I have found referred staff members tend to stay longer because they have been recruited and integrated into the organization by my top performers.

One of my colleagues, Bill Eggbeer, used a successful strategy while he was with Manor Care. He had potential new employees spend part of a shift working with high performing staff as a way to sample the work as well as serve as part of the selection process. New hires are assigned to high performing mentors to provide strong role modeling during the critical first 60 days of employment.

Job Fairs

Job Fairs are challenging and time-consuming, so be sure to set the event date far enough in advance to allow adequate time for planning. Mondays and Fridays are usually not good days for job fairs. Depending on the positions you are looking to fill, consider a job fair on a Saturday or in the evening so those potential candidates currently working can attend. It may be advantageous to take part in a larger, local job fair before trying to execute your own.

A mass mailing of an invitation in the form of a flyer, postcard or letter allows you to reach the largest number of candidates with the least expenditure of time and money. Mail by zip code to the geographical area where you know your current employees live and spend time. Also ask your current staff to promote the fair to their family and friends. Offer incentives or raffle prizes to attendees to encourage them to attend or stop by your booth.

A job fair is a great vehicle to personally assess candidates. Be sure to take the time to screen and interview candidates on the spot. The best predictors of success are a track record of high energy and team leadership, and some level of comparable past performance. The likelihood of success is high for candidates with this profile, especially if they have a strong ability to adapt and produce in a new environment.

Asking about four to eight major past accomplishments in a patterned question format is the key to this type of interviewing approach. The accomplishments need to involve individual, team, and job specific efforts. When combined with fact-finding, these questions can reveal all the important details of each accomplishment. By asking only four questions, this type of profile can be determined for *any* candidate. The questions are listed below and included in the Appendix:

Question 1: Please describe your most significant accomplishment or please tell me what you are most proud of. Ask the candidate about his or her last two or three jobs and listen for personal energy and impact. Use fact-finding to get lots of examples and details — when, how, why, impact, results and time frame. Measure the trends over time.

Question 2: Tell me about your most important team accomplishment, or about a great team you have been on. Look for team work and/or team leadership during the last two or three jobs. Get examples of the candidate's actual role, time and effort involved, interpersonal challenges and motivation, and conflict resolution skills.

Question 3: One of our key principal accountabilities for this position is _____. Tell me about a time when you did something similar. Look for job-specific competency and get the details to minimize exaggeration. Anchor each major principal accountability with a past accomplishment.

Question 4: If you were to get this job, how would you go about implementing and organizing _____ (describe project). Look for adaptability and ability to contribute in a new environment. Ask about the top two or three principal accountabilities.

Be prepared to make preliminary job offers to exceptional candidates with the caveat of background checks and references. You don't want to lose an exceptional candidate.

Conferences/Professional Associations

Participation in conferences and professional associations provide an opportunity to promote your organization as well as learn from other professionals what they're doing to recruit and retain staff members.

In addition, you should identify some of the key players in your community and forward a list of your job openings to them on a regular basis. Solicit their knowledge of candidates to fill open positions in your organization.

Resources Guide

CHAPTER 6

Underpaid Professions/Overlooked Resource Pools: Attracting those looking for a career change

There is no doubt the job market is extremely tight. Why? Because we are all fighting for the same top employees by running the same ads in the same newspapers. But there is a more direct approach to hiring good people. Look for people in professions that have similar skill-sets.

Many professions have well-educated people looking for change and a different career. With a good training program, you can fill your job needs with many of these types of workers.

Take, for example, teachers. A teacher's skill-set is often well-suited for a department head position in assisted living. Teachers with fewer than five years experience typically make less than $30,000. A salary of $30,000 and a little more could easily be accommodated within the assisted living profession.

So, how you are going to attract this pool of prospective employees? Post an ad in monthly trade magazines for educators or create an ad for an on-line education-oriented employment Web site.

What should you include in the ad to encourage applicants? Much thought has to be given to developing a plan to attract other professionals, but with some ingenuity, it's possible to deduce correlating attributes and job skills.

Other prospective employees may be found in the mental-health, childcare, law enforcement and social services industries as well as the military. Be creative and widen your scope to find well-skilled employees in similar and often overlooked markets.

One of the problems with traditional recruiting efforts is employers are conducting them in a *laissez-faire*, routine fashion, doing the same thing over and over again and — for some reason — expecting different results. We advertise in the classifieds, we put out our "Help Wanted" signs and we get the same useless results as always. Instead of the same old rigmarole, why not try something new? Let me share a couple of creative resources that could be useful.

Returning to the Workforce

In many realms, the college-educated 40-year-old homemaker is seen as an ideal prospective employee, but they're considered fairly unattainable. Actually, it just takes ingenuity and flexibility to find and attract them. Flex time, compressed workweeks and job sharing are very attractive to this group. One of the best retention philosophies for these women is whether they sense they can attend to their personal life and still develop in the company. The simple act of changing a work shift to coincide with the end of the school day

The simple act of changing a work shift to coincide with the end of the school day could make your company this demographic group's employer of choice.

could make your company this demographic group's employer of choice.

Getting the Best Young Worker

My daughter, Ashley, was a national finalist in a business club known as DECA (Distributive Education Clubs of America). Formed more than 50 years ago, DECA is an association for students interested in marketing, management and entrepreneurial business. DECA prepares students for the business world through competitions based on real-life business scenarios.

I was recently asked to be a judge for a state DECA competition. When I arrived at the upscale convention center, I was shocked at the number of attendees. Over 2,000 young people from all over the state were to be judged in the competition. I was amazed by the number of bright, well-dressed, well-mannered kids participating in the event. As I spoke with some of the young adults, my enthusiasm soared; I felt as though I had just hit the motherlode of young workers!

I gave detailed information about my company to several of the participants. Some eagerly asked whether I would ever consider giving someone like them a job. I'd struck gold!

All of us conduct many interviews in the course of our careers and we are — more often than not — disappointed with the caliber of people we get. Nevertheless, here I was, sitting with more than 2,000 kids who had been coached on how to act and dress when participating in the business world. They had been put through the rigors of knowing how to interact with management staff on a conversational level. It was obvious they had been taught the concepts of business and wanted to learn more. Almost all of them were college-bound.

As I spoke with them about the assisted living and senior housing industry, it was apparent they were interested in a business that had a social conscience. These were kids that did not care as much whether they made $7-an-hour or $9-an-hour. They cared more about what they could learn from the experience. Clearly, these were goal-oriented teenagers who were going to leverage their job experiences into future careers. I was so excited I immediately called our Vice President of Human Resources to come to the conference and witness this amazing labor pool.

In the briefing session that instructs judges about their responsibilities, I scanned the room and studied the other judges' name tags and the companies they represented. Some of the judges were clearly parents who had agreed to help their local high school. Yet it was also apparent that many organizations were way ahead of me in recognizing DECA and seeing it as a gigantic recruiting opportunity. Obviously, they targeted this organization in their strategic plan for recruitment.

Retail chains such as The Gap and Eddie Bauer were represented. Some even had booths describing the merits of their companies. The most impressive group representation, though, was by the U.S. Marine Corps which was also the most aggressive of the lot. It was no accident that out of the one hundred judges, 10 were Marines dressed to the nines in full uniform. Their mission, obviously, was to recruit from this talented and pre-qualified field of young people. In conversation with one of the Marines, I learned the conference served as public service duty, but recruiting a couple of smart young people into the

Corps would be a bonus. There was no doubt the emphasis was on the latter.

Volunteers

Volunteers can enhance the services that you provide, strengthen your community involvement, and enrich your exposure to certain communities. Many companies lose volunteers, though, because they don't create a valuable experience for them or they don't fully utilize their skills.

Just like a paid employee, volunteers must be provided with challenge and motivation for continued success. Lay out the responsibilities of each job. Plan training and support programs to facilitate volunteer learning and development, and ensure that volunteers are aware of the goals and outcome objectives for their involvement. Be honest about the workload and time commitment.

Comprehensive orientation and volunteer training programs give volunteers a feeling of belonging and status. It shows that the organization values them enough to make an investment in them and, again, helps to reinforce their commitment to the cause. Orientation also helps set the tone of the work area and allows volunteers to adapt more easily to the organization's surroundings.

Volunteers are not driven by a paycheck, but rather recognition. Recognition programs show that your organization values volunteer support. They also provide a motivation for continuing commitment from your volunteers.

Alternative Sources of Employees

We have spoken much about being creative with your hiring practices in today's economy. One such creative mechanism is the alternative employee. They exist in many fashions. If welfare reform has taught us anything, it is that most people would rather work than take handouts.

Looking for a Second Chance

An often overlooked group of prospective employees are those people looking to put their lives back together or who need a second chance. I was recently at a fundraiser for the prevention of domestic violence. There were hundreds of people in attendance. Several women who had lived in the domestic violence shelters were sharing their stories. One of the board members of this particular domestic violence chapter sat at my table. I asked him to tell me about the women living in the shelter. How long do they stay there? What kinds of things do they do? Did they have regular jobs? Did the shelter organize specific activities for their benefit?

He explained that sometimes victims of domestic violence are forced to leave their regular jobs out of fear the person who is abusing them may track them down at work. The women are welcome to stay in these shelters for months. In fact, one woman was in this shelter for more than a year.

The women are usually between jobs, not really wanting to go out and apply for something while they are in transition, the board member explained. While they are usually involved in some kind of case management that involves physical and mental health programs as well as legal advocacy and employment training, their time is confined to the shelter.

My experience with these women indicates they would make great temporary employees. Additionally, the benefit of helping and caring for someone might be very beneficial to their own recovery process. Having a sense of purpose and pride in accomplishment could enhance their own self-esteem.

It might be a worthwhile and valuable experience to contact local domestic violence and/or homeless shelters to see if some residents might be interested in working with you. Since confidentiality is key to their immediate living situation, you'll want to investigate how you can best protect these women and minimize their fear of being in public. Also have an emergency plan in place should an abusive spouse show up and cause a commotion. Although this idea comes with some unique challenges, it could really turn into a win-win situation.

Following is a listing of other alternative resource pools:

Department of Corrections — Could your next employee be an ex-convict? Almost every prison throughout the country offers some kind of educational program to help prison inmates. This can include everything from academic degree programs to religious studies. The basic idea behind most vocational programs in state prisons is reform. According to several sources and justice statistics, prisoners who have taken part in vocational courses are less likely to return to prison.

These programs are aimed at helping ex-convicts rebuild their life by establishing vocational and educational skills, support systems and independent living skills prior to entering the community.

Most prisons have Community Release Programs or Work Release Programs which you can access through your state's Department of Corrections.

United Way — By contacting your local United Way, you can find non-profit organizations that specialize in rehabilitating and re-training quality candidates for the workforce. The list of pools would include homeless and/or domestic violence shelters (as discussed above), displaced homemakers programs, career transition workshops, developmentally disabled training, drug and alcohol recovery programs, etc. After completion of expert programs, candidates have marketable skills, tools for life and a place of belonging in the community. You can access your local United Way through their Web site: www.unitedway.org

Work Opportunity Tax Credit (WOTC) — The WOTC is a federal income tax credit that encourages private sector employers to hire eight targeted groups of job seekers. The tax incentive is designed to help the job seekers most in need of employment opportunities that allow them to gain on-the-job experience thereby helping them move towards economic self-sufficiency. The WOTC can reduce employers' federal tax liability by as much as $2,400 per new hire.

By calling 1-877-828-2050 (a toll-free number), employers and other interested parties can conveniently obtain the required WOTC/WtW (Welfare to Work) tax credit request forms and State contact information. This Fax-On-Demand service allows access to WOTC/WtW request forms via fax by using a touch-tone telephone or a fax machine. Or visit the Employment and Training Administration Web site (below).

The Employment and Training Administration (ETA) — The ETA seeks to build up the labor market through the training of the workforce and the placement of workers in jobs through employment services. This Web site is designed to direct adults, youth, dislocated workers, and workforce development professionals to information on these programs and services. Employers will find information on several areas, including tax credits and other hiring incentives, how to find and train employees, assistance with plant closures and downsizing, legislation text, and ETA grants and contracts.

Contact information: www.doleta.gov/programs/

Workforce Investment Act — The Workforce Investment Act was passed by Congress in the late 1990s and launched One-Stop Centers that combine education, training and employment programs in a central location. These Centers are replacing the older Private Industry Council (PIC) programs and are already up and running in thirty states. Services are free to both the employer and the candidate.

Contact information: www.ttrc.doleta.gov/onestop/

Temporary Assistance for Needy Families (TANF) — TANF provides assistance and work opportunities to needy families by granting states the federal funds and wide flexibility to develop and implement their own welfare program. The Office of Family Assistance oversees this program. This and other relevant programs can be found on the U.S. Department of Health and Human Services' Web site: www.hhs.gov

Center for Employment Training (CET) — CET provides low-income, hard-to-serve individuals with marketable vocational educational training and supportive services that will contribute to their achieving economic self-sufficiency. CET's goal for each participant is permanent, unsubsidized job placement with good benefits and growth potential. Vocational training is integrated with life skills instruction and workplace acculturation classes. Employment supports and extensive follow-up services are also provided to participants.

CET's headquarters at the San Jose campus oversees a national network of 30 vocational educational centers in 11 states (including CA-16 sites, CT, DC, IL, NV, NJ, NC, PA, TX, VA, WA).

Contact information: CET Corporate Offices, 701 Vine St., San Jose, CA 95110, (408) 287-7924 or call 1-800-533-2519 for your local center.

Wider Opportunities for Women (WOW) — WOW works nationally and in its home community of Washington, DC to achieve economic independence and equality of opportunity for women and girls. For more than 35 years, WOW has helped women learn to earn, with programs emphasizing literacy, technical and nontraditional skills, welfare-to-work transition, and career development. Visit their Web site, WOWonline.org, to learn more about their national programs, Work4women and Workplace Solutions.

Hire a Vet — Hire a Vet is a Women's Research and Education Institute (REI) project, which has been undertaken in conjunction with the Department of Labor. The goal of the program is to encourage employers to hire women veterans. Women veterans are skilled and dependable workers — often trained at taxpayers' expense — so hiring women veterans allows employers to reap the benefits of that training.

Contact information: http://www. wrei.org/ military/ women_veterans/

Vet Jobs — VetJobs.com was established from three years of Internet research on job and résumé sites. This research indicated there was a gap in sites which assisted recruiters in identifying not only transitioning military, but also highly qualified veterans who have separated over the decades and are now productive members of the civilian work force in all disciplines.

Studies have shown that at least 60 percent (some say higher) of military personnel who transition to the civilian sector are under-employed for up to four years after separation. This is frequently because the hiring companies do not fully appreciate the capabilities of a person who has served in the military due to incorrect perceptions or the military person was not fully knowledgeable of how to approach the civilian job market.

Contact information: 1000 Johnson Ferry Road, Suite E-150, Marietta, GA 30068, 1-877-VetJobs, www.vetjobs.com

Senior Job Bank.org — Senior Job Bank exists to spread the word about the wisdom of keeping our older population in the workforce longer. The Senior Job Bank Web site offers an easy, effective and free method for our senior citizens to find occasional, part-time, flexible, temporary and even full-time jobs.

Contact information: www.seniorjobbank.org

Experience Works! — Experience Works is the first nationwide staffing service specifically designed for mature workers. It helps older workers find jobs that match their skills, abilities, and work preferences, and help employers fill their temporary, temp-to-perm and permanent full-and part-time employment needs with reliable, skilled, and experienced workers.

Whether they are re-entering the job market, seeking a career change, or just finding retirement a bore, these candidates can bring not only experience and skill to the workplace, but qualities and attitudes that are hard to find, such as loyalty, honesty, dedication, hard work, good judgment and commitment to service.

Contact information: www.Experienceworks.org

America's Job Bank — America's Job Bank is a database of electronic résumés, which have been put into the system by individuals seeking job opportunities. The system is designed so that you as an employer can search those electronic résumés to find qualified employees.

Contact information: www.americasjobbank.com

Snag A Job — Snagajob.com specializes in high school and college students' part-time summer jobs and internships.

Contact information: www.snagajob.com

VolunteerMatch — VolunteerMatch utilizes the power of the Internet to help individuals nationwide find volunteer opportunities posted by local non-profit and public sector organizations.

VolunteerMatch's powerful online database allows volunteers to search thousands of one-time and ongoing opportunities by zip code, category, and date. Contributing organizations post their own opportunities, giving volunteers easy access to an accurate and diverse source of activities.

VolunteerMatch is available nationwide. It benefits from strong local support in San Francisco, San Jose, Seattle, Boston, Washington, D.C., Charlotte, New York, and Los Angeles.

Contact information: www.Volunteermatch.org

National Retiree Volunteer Coalition (NRVC) — NRVC's mission is to advance retiree leadership and service as a corporate, community and national asset.

Contact information: Volunteers of America, 1660 Duke Street, Alexandria, VA 22314, (800) 899-0089, www.nrvc.org

Be sure to also use your state's resources as well. For example, in the state of Washington, we have the Washington State Employment Security Department as well as the Washington State Diversity Network. These sites have other important employment links.

Also note that government programs — while numerous — can vary from state to state. In addition, it's important to check early in the process as to reporting requirements and other conditions. Sometimes, these can be quite rigorous and more than a typical administrative staff can master.

Hiring
CHAPTER 7

The Screening Process

There are several books with thousands of strategies for screening employees. They include complicated testing processes, psychological analysis and even handwriting analysis for personality traits.

The best initial screening test I have found for a potential candidate is the first phone call to the company. When we place an advertisement in the paper for a position — whether it is for a line staff member or senior manager — we always include our phone number in the ad. The likelihood someone will apply is substantially higher when your phone number is included in the ad since people want instant access to more information. Your job hotline phone number can put the candidate in direct contact with a person who can give the specifics of the position.

Some time ago I was troubleshooting for an assisted living home. We were in desperate need of care managers to run the building. The home had never placed an ad with a telephone number. When the telephone number was finally placed in the ad, the phone started ringing off the hook much to the chagrin of the receptionist who commented, "I think putting our telephone number in the ad is a dumb idea. I cannot get any work done with all the calls."

I explained to her that she had an exceptional problem. We were losing thousands of dollars a day in revenue because we did not have the staff to accommodate our residents' needs. The moral of this story is you need to explain your reasoning clearly and coach the person who answers these calls so that they understand the significance of the task.

Your receptionist can be key in screening applicants. Make sure the person taking calls has a copy of the ad. Then, teach that individual to write down a score or grade with a few comments about how each potential applicant interacted over the phone. It is surprising how rude people can be to staff who answer the telephone. In fact, I frequently will answer our corporate office telephone without giving my name. I am constantly surprised at how people treat the phone receptionist as an inconsequential and unintelligent drone. Therefore, we give the power to our receptionist to score these people. We get amazing first impression insights from these calls allowing us to weed out the phonies for the interview process.

Interview Preparation

Too often in the interview process, we, as employers, become lackadaisical with our preparation. We are then very surprised when we do not get the caliber of people we want. A simple way around this is to know and convey your specific expectations.

What kind of expectations should you have? Let's start simple. Have you identified the core competencies of the job? What are the critical skills that one must have in order to meet the job requirements? We usually tend to do this well with jobs that have clear, quantifiable goals. For example, when you set out to hire a secretary, you may specifically seek a person capable of typing 80 words per minute or who has experience working with certain software. Unfortunately, we are less attentive when it comes to skills that are not as easily quantified.

Let me be more specific. When I hire an executive director for an assisted living home, I want that person to be able to speak in public. Although it may seem like an obvious qualification for the job, it's rarely indicated in job postings. Some think that speaking in front of large groups of people is a tall order. Is it imperative that the executive director be able to address a group of perhaps 100? Yes. How else would they communicate with their staff, or at large promotional events? Therefore, it is also imperative that the job description identifies public speaking as a requirement.

Before you conduct your interview, give your candidates a "heads up" on the culture of your company. Corporate cultures are all over the board these days. If your company is relaxed, frowning on blue suits and brown shoes, then relay that information to the candidate before she/he arrives. Conversely, tell the candidate if you have a strict dress code. Don't make your candidate guess whether it will be a "Casual Friday," "Business Monday" or "Sporty Wednesday" type of company. It is not fair to leave them guessing and possibly dress inappropriately. Be up front. You and the candidate will likely be more comfortable during the interview process.

Make sure you provide candidates with directions to the interview location. This suggestion may seem overly simplistic, but I constantly hear of candidates missing interviews just because they couldn't find their way. Make sure all interviewees receive clear, typed directions to avoid any confusion. In addition, candidates should be supplied with a contact person's name and number in case they need to cancel the appointment, call for directions en route or inform someone they're running late.

With unemployment levels as low as they have been, it is likely most candidates will be employed elsewhere, and will need to leave their current place of employment for their scheduled interview. Allow them to be responsible to their current employers by telling them how long your interview process will take. I always like to overestimate. I tell people the group interview process will take four hours, although it normally runs three to three-and-a-half hours. It is terribly distracting to the whole group interview process to have a candidate get up and leave before the conclusion.

Finally, let the candidates know what your next step will be. Whether that means you will call them later that day or the following week, let them know when a decision will be made. Also, let them know if you need more information to make your decision such as reference letters and phone numbers, licenses and so forth.

By keeping your candidate fully informed, they will be better prepared and more at ease. Remember that they are interviewing you as much you are interviewing them. A little thoughtfulness goes a long way.

Digging for the Hidden Skills

Recruiting and interviewing are more marketing than selling. If you over-sell, over-talk, and under-listen you'll either lose the best candidates or pay too much. From this point on, you won't learn anything about the candidate other than what she/he wants you to know. When you talk more than the candidate does, you actually lose control of the interview. Even in an extremely competitive labor market, you can create a compelling opportunity and make the candidate earn the job. When you do this, candidates will sell you.

Today, even line staff applicants are coached in the art of being interviewed. High schools are teaching students what employers look for in the interview process. Business clubs such as the Future Business Leaders of America (FBLA) and Distributive Education Clubs of America (DECA) are coaching kids to answer questions the proper way.

My 19-year-old daughter has been through more than 30 interviews in the last four years. All this practice enables employment seekers to present themselves as very polished candidates because they know just how to answer questions to please a potential employer.

The Group Interview

So how do you cull the wheat from the chaff? How do you learn more about the candidate's personality and job skills yet stay within the legal confines of the interview process? How do you detect a team player? How do you ask and obtain valid information on non-quantifiable skills?

The answer is that you test for it. No, I'm not suggesting you give someone a written examination on sensitivity. I am talking about conducting an experiment, an interviewing experiment. This experiment is in the form of a group interview. The group interview process presents a laboratory where scenarios are prepared and there is no rehearsed answer that can be given. In fact, the real information does not come in the form of the candidates' answers as much as it does from the reaction of the group to some of the answers. The candid reaction to the stimuli offers very valuable information.

I was first introduced to the group interview process in 1992 while working in Seattle, Washington. The theory was introduced at a traveling one-day training session that charged attendees $100. The session purported group interviews would save time and allow employers to experience group dynamics. Although my introduction to the process at this session was less than memorable, I found the concept of group dynamics in employment interviews extremely fascinating. I have tweaked and reworked the process after interviewing groups in this manner. This process is a vital key to discovering superior employees.

My first experiments were simple. I tested for traits such as initiative. I did the "glass-of-water test." If we had 14 candidates being interviewed at once, I would put 11 glasses on the table. After I had asked a few questions, I would then ask everyone to take a glass of water.

This simple experiment gave some amazing information. Some people would selfishly climb over each other for a glass of water. What does this say about someone? It implies this person is selfish and must win at all costs, a looking-out-for-number-one type person.

Others would get a glass of water and then offer it to their fellow candidate. What does this say? This is probably a giving, unselfish team player that works for the good of the whole.

Still others would notice they had not been fast enough to grab a glass and so they sit staring at their shoes in embarrassment. What does this say about the person? Quiet and withdrawn — probably wouldn't be the first person to bring a problem to your attention. Last, there is always the person who will say, "Excuse me, Mr. Clark. Obviously, someone has mistaken the number of attendees because we seem to be a few glasses short. If you tell me where I could get some more glasses of water, I will be willing to get some for my teammates." What does this tell you about the candidate? A self-starter who has initiative, a person who shows leadership skills, a person not afraid to stand up in a crowd, point out a problem and find a solution.

Most people think group interviews are done to save time. Although seeing several candidates at one time can be time efficient, it is not the primary reason why I do group interviews. The reason is purely to discover information about candidates that I could never obtain from a one-on-one interview. It is extremely difficult, if not impossible, for candidates to know what I am going to ask in a group interview. The questions are not routine ones and are purposely meant to be disarming.

Realize that everything you do with candidates can elicit some bit of telling information. I often walk into the meeting room five minutes late. In the meantime, I plant a staff member among the candidates before introductions are made. The interviewees assume the staff member is just another candidate. The designated staff member is there to see how people interact with each other — are they friendly, are they smug, what do they ask, etc. It always amazes me how people may badmouth the company one minute and then when the "suit" walks in, the same people talk about how great the company is and how honored they are to be there. I am not advocating being deceitful, I am simply suggesting a strategic observation and information-gathering tactic before putting all your cards on the table. In this way, people will volunteer valuable information without being asked.

Setting Up the Group Interview

The format is simple. Nevertheless, there are some basic protocols to follow. The group should consist of 10 to 15 people applying for the same job. With a group of less than 10, the group dynamics tend to disappear. More than fifteen and you will not be able to keep accurate notes on the dynamics.

Candidates should be informed ahead of time that they are going to be interviewed in a group. Most candidates have some hesitation about this process. You need to have a skilled person telling them what the process is all about. It is not uncommon for candidates to think that you are trying to rope them into something that has to do with tiered sales. I remember one candidate saying, "You are not going to try and have me sell cleaning products to my friends and family are you?"

Again, most candidates think you are doing the exercise to save time. One candidate wrote me a nasty letter when she heard she was going to be interviewed in a group format. The gist of the letter was she thought interviewing a group would not allow her the attention she deserved given her qualifications. Once I had explained the process to her she inquired, "Is it too late to participate? The process sounds fascinating."

Our human resources staff is extremely skilled at reassuring people the interview will be a positive experience. In fact, we frequently get letters from candidates who went through this process and said it was the best and most intriguing interview experience of their life. Some of the candidates have even made lasting friendships with their fellow interviewees. Here's some of the feedback I have received after using this process:

Even though I did not expect to enjoy the process, I did!

I loved it; a lot more enjoyable and informative than your traditional one-on-one interview. On top of that, I felt it gave me a chance to show one of the things I'm good at — working with and leading a team. I loved the chance to get feedback in a more casual atmosphere. Though professional, it was more laid back, like me.

I loved the group interview process. It is great to get to know others, especially knowing who I'm up against for this position. The group interview is also fun and made me feel more comfortable in the interview process.

Why? The explanation is very simple: We interview in a group format to garner information that presents itself only in group dynamics. In addition, these people tend to already have the same skills, talents and interest in a similar career position.

Schedule more candidates than you would like to have attend. There will be some fallout between people agreeing to attend and those who actually show up. It has been my experience that attendance results depend largely on the skill level of the position for which you are interviewing. When I interview for a senior management position, I usually plan on a 15 percent fallout. Therefore, if I want 14 in the group I will likely schedule 16. If I am interviewing for line staff, the fallout is much greater — usually more than 30 percent.

Some of this fallout can be minimized by having a staff member call to schedule the candidate's interview several days out and then place another call to remind and confirm the appointment with the candidate a day or two before the interview. Always inform the candidate that if they should change their mind, they should call you so someone else can have their spot to interview. Again, you do not want to end up scheduling 10 people and have only six show up. The group interview process then becomes ineffective.

The Meeting Place

After confirming the candidates' attendance, be certain to hold the interview in a place free of interruptions. I like to hold interviews in hotel meeting rooms or private clubs where distractions are minimized. When you are in your office environment, the temptation to take an important telephone call or deal with an urgent matter is much greater. But, if your options are limited, pick the quietest room available and instruct staff not to interrupt you.

Make sure there is room to roam. The room should accommodate up to 15 interviewees, three to four evaluators, and a facilitator. If the room is too cramped, it may change the dynamics of your interview. People get very nervous when you invade their personal space. Chairs ideally should be 12 to 18 inches apart and should be placed in a circle. I have placed chairs around a table but prefer a circle of chairs, because you can read more body language. A shaky foot, clenched fists or a nervous twitch can be concealed under a conference table.

The meeting spot should also accommodate three to four breakout groups. The groups should not be within earshot of each other. Groups may need to meet in a small alcove or in other rooms in the building. If the room is big enough, they can meet in different corners of the room.

The Group Convenes

When people come in, it is important to have nametags waiting for them. A company greeter should hand out the nametags and direct the candidates to the appropriate room.

The pre-interview time is extremely valuable. You will discover much about the candidates whom you are about to interview. Watch for the person who comes in the door complaining, "This place was so hard to find, I don't know why anyone would have an interview here." Or the excuse maker, "The reason I am late is that there was an old lady driving 15 mph in front of me. I don't know why they allow people like that to have a license."

Look for the people who go out of their way to introduce themselves to the other candidates or try to make others feel comfortable. Leadership qualities often manifest at this stage. Is there a candidate who pulls out his interview letter to instruct others on what they are about to encounter while others wonder out loud about the process? This indicates someone who is well-prepared, structured and assertive.

People cannot fake who they are all the time. Often the best time to get job information is when people do not really think they are being interviewed.

Employer Roles

There are two roles for the employer to play during the course of the interview. One is the role of a facilitator and the other is a role of an evaluator. Both roles are critically important. The facilitator's role is to be the conductor of the experiment. He needs to be in tune with the temperament of the crowd. He needs to know when to infuse humor and when to take the group down a serious road. He is also in charge of the energy of the group. Since group interviews can last up to three-and-a-half hours, conserving the energy of the group is vital.

The last duty is that of time management since group interviews can easily go several hours. Once you pass the three hour mark you tend to burn people out. Three hours will go by very quickly. You may also be surprised at how draining a process like this can be for all participants.

The evaluators for the group are assigned four-to-five candidates to watch and document their reactions and behavior. Again, the power of the group interview is in observing the behavior of the candidates when they are "off camera." Make sure the evaluators are spread evenly around the room. We usually have evaluators pick four candidates in a row who are sitting directly in front of them. Doing this makes it very natural for evaluators to observe the candidates. Evaluators then take notes not only on the comments that their candidates make, but also observe the candidates while others are talking. Is the candidate rude or disinterested while someone else talks? What is their body language saying? How do the other candidates react when this person speaks?

The Interview Process

The interview begins with all staff introducing themselves by their first name only. They may also tell a little about themselves personally. We try to stay away from giving titles and job descriptions. I have done it both ways, but I have found that candidates try to play up to the most senior member in the room when they know each staff member's position within the company. This changes the dynamics for the group. Sometimes candidates know who you are, so this point becomes moot. It is still helpful if the rest of the staff's titles remain anonymous.

Our interview process is usually a three-step process after the screening of résumés. The first group interview is to see if candidates really possess the basic skills and cultural fit for the company. This first round may consist of two to three groups of 15 candidates. These groups are then usually narrowed down to a final group interview of 12 to 15 candidates. The second group interview narrows down the skills and matches the candidates' talents with the job requirements. At times, you may not have enough candidates to have a first and second round of interviews. Consequently, you want to structure the one group interview to include both a cultural fit and a skills-assessment.

The one-on-one interview should be reserved for candidates that you are 90 percent certain you would hire. It is just a matter of choosing the best fit for the job. Three to four candidates are selected to do a one-on-one interview as finalists. After the entire process, the most appropriate candidate should emerge as the best person for the job.

Your questions should differ in each round, becoming more finite with each consecutive round, so that by the time you get to the one-on-one, the candidate should be answering very skill-set-oriented questions.

In the initial round, the facilitator should have the candidates introduce and tell a little about themselves immediately after the staff introductions. A couple of important points need to be made here. First, start with a candidate you think has the energy and enthusiasm to volunteer information eagerly. The facilitator needs to pick a candidate who will set the tone for information gathering. You will be very surprised at how the preceding response greatly influences the next.

The other rule is to set a time limit, usually a minute or so, for each response. Some candidates believe they will never have enough time to talk, so they will try to dominate the time and the group. Be firm about keeping people on schedule even if it means cutting people off. As long as you warn them about the rules, they should respect them.

The last rule benefits the evaluator's role. Tell people to state their name prior to answering every question. When interviewing numerous candidates, it is easy to become confused with their names. Some candidates may even look very much alike, thus adding to the confusion.

I usually ask no more than four to five questions during the interview. Remember that if each candidate takes just two minutes to answer a question, it can take 30 minutes to answer one question. Limit side talk or you will be there all day long.

I have two questions I always ask near the end of the interview. The first is very powerful and requires an incredible amount of sensitivity. I ask the candidate to tell me about the most difficult decision they have ever had to make in their life. I then start to qualify the question, telling the candidates, "I am not looking for you to say the decision between math and history as your major in college. I am looking for a gut-wrenching decision that you still may ponder over from time to time. This decision may even have been life-changing in nature."

You also want to warn the candidates to only offer information with which they are completely comfortable. Tell them that preference points are not earned by giving the most dramatic information. Remind all the candidates what they hear during this time in the interview should be kept confidential and not shared with others outside of the group. This explanation is necessary and gives the candidates time to contemplate their answers.

The next thing the facilitator does is vital to the success of the question — choosing a person to go first. Often, I will ask for a volunteer who I know will give an in-depth answer. Again, this person sets the tone for the entire group. By this time in the interview, the facilitator should know who might give such a response. If this person gives an answer along the lines of choosing to disconnect the life-support system for a parent, the remaining candidates' answers will have a similar depth of content. Try to stay away from the candidate whose hand always shoots up first or the one who may not seem to be respected by the group.

During this point in the interview, it is a very serious and often emotional time. I have felt honored being privy to the stories shared with me during this process. There have been women who decided to report a rape, people who had to come to grips with bad relationships, people who made decisions about a variety of addictions they or a loved one had in their life, and so on.

Why in the world do I subject candidates to these types of questions? Well, first of all, people will only share what they want to share. Remember that they get no extra points for drama. It's important for me, though, because my staff in assisted living deals with very difficult issues every day — residents who die, residents who are put on life support, and families who have a tough time dealing with what is happening to their parents. These are daily events for our staff members. A traditional interview process will not elicit the responses necessary to determine how people will handle major life issues, so, I test for it. I can test for sensitivity and compassion in this process. When you see a person offer the tearful storyteller a tissue, you're witnessing compassion. When you see another candidate give the person a hug, you're seeing sensitivity.

I have been asked if I would ask this type of question when interviewing engineers. Engineers may give different answers, but I think it is extremely valuable to see how people handle situations that make them uncomfortable. You may not be testing to see how sensitive someone is, but seeing how someone handles adversity is always valuable. So the answer is, yes, do it and see what information comes from the process.

After this round of questions, I believe it is imperative to acknowledge each individual for the courage it took to give the answer. Again, this portion of the interview can be draining and you want to express your appreciation.

Finally, the last question I always ask is "Which person in this room would you hire besides yourself?" This is a written response that can gain amazing results. No matter how good your evaluators are, they will miss something, whether good or bad. Of course, it is always possible to miss the bad because candidates make the extra effort to hide it. Nevertheless, by asking this final question, you have just turned the interviewees into interviewers. You now have 15 more opinions to weigh against your own.

Finally, the last question I always ask is "Which person in this room would you hire besides yourself?"

You will be surprised by the information provided by the candidates. I was once interviewing to fill administrator positions and one gentleman was acing the process. When it came time to read whom the candidates would hire not one of the 14 voted for him. There must be some mistake, I thought; he appears to be the natural choice. Maybe this is a conspiracy to force me not to hire the best person. As I continued to read through the responses, I noticed three of the candidates had put little narratives after their vote. Their narratives described why my favorite candidate was not their choice. They saw the candidate shining during the interview process but they also saw the condescending way he treated some of the other candidates. One candidate reported that this candidate made highly derogatory remarks about the interview process, but then raved how creative the process was when the staff was present. This candidate sailed through the entire process until that final and critical step. The other candidates actually prevented me from making a potentially bad hire.

Breakout Sessions

Regardless of the position for which you are hiring, I believe it is vital to have a smaller breakout session, approximately one-and-a-half hours into the group interview. For practical purposes, this session allows for a restroom break and stretching time, but it also allows for a different dynamic. The information in these small groups of four-to-five people is of great significance. Split the groups any way you wish. Sometimes I merely ask people to count off by four or I might separate the dominant personalities. Again, this is where the facilitator's assessment of the group personality comes in handy.

Give each group a scenario on which you would like them to work. This scenario should directly relate to the core competencies of the job. For instance, I may give a group of potential managers a profit and loss statement from one of my buildings, then give them some financial goals for the building, asking them for a plan to achieve the goals. Obviously, you can give a variety of skill screenings depending upon the job for which you are interviewing. You can have a customer service scenario, a medical scenario or an employee issue scenario to name a few. I then send the groups on their way to a private area and ask them to choose a spokesperson to present their solution to the whole group in 30 minutes.

I am always surprised when some people who have touted their strength in financial management look befuddled when presented with this exercise. The real truths come out when the group starts to interact. Evaluators rotate between groups and quietly take notes. Immediately, the exercise of group dynamics is put into motion. People will jockey for position as leader of the group; others play a role of consensus makers, while some become very passive. Some candidates will demand they be the spokesperson. Periodically, evaluators will come by and remind the group how much time is left. This element of stress is introduced to see how people will work together to meet the demands of the job. The personality traits relinquished during this process will be overtly detected.

When all the breakout groups reconvene, it is interesting to listen to the spokesperson's presentation. Don't just listen for the answer to the scenario question (there may not be one right answer) but attend to how the answer is presented. You'll also be able to determine whether the spokesperson was elected by popular vote or was self-appointed. Listen carefully to the words the spokesperson uses. Does she/he start the sentence with, "I thought we should just raise the rents?" I had an experience like this before and I have always been successful with this philosophy: the frequent use of "I" shows selfishness and lack of team spirit.

The best-case scenario unfolds when someone stands up and says, "I represent Team One, which was made up of Larry, Helen, George and Stan. They have graciously elected me as their spokesperson. Now Helen has a great idea of auditing our food costs. Stan also has a great strategy of going back and seeing if we can lower our property taxes. Is there anything else my group would like to offer that I may have overlooked?"

This type of response offers insight into who is a team player, who builds consensus, who is secure in their knowledge and knows how to motivate others. Observe how others in the team are reacting to the spokesperson's presentation. Are they nodding in agreement or trying to jump in to say their piece? A lot of information is gathered from just a few sentences. This is a great leadership exercise.

Wrapping It Up

When you wrap up the interview, thank people for their time. Let them know when you will be making your decision and how they will be contacted. Contact each candidate regardless of whether or not you intend to hire them. These people have just become salespeople for your company. Be courteous.

Group interviews are not the end-all, be-all to interviewing. I am not suggesting that you hire someone based solely on whether they offer to get someone a glass of water, but the information you gather from this process is most effective when used in its entirety. Look for patterns of behavior during the interview. Remember that the interview is a fact-finding experiment. These facts are merely one piece of your decision-making process. You should still screen applications and résumés carefully. You should still conduct a one-on-one interview with each finalist. You should still perform diligent reference checking. However, the difference between this process and the more traditional interview process is the additional behavioral information not usually acquired.

After the interview, the evaluators and the facilitator should get together. Do this immediately following the interview so observations are fresh in your mind. I have tried to rekindle my thoughts and comments a day later and it was a disaster. It is very difficult to remember who said what. The group usually starts out by saying which candidate they would never hire. This usually eliminates the bottom half of the candidates. Then, we decide on the top three or four candidates. The evaluators, though responsible for only a few candidates, naturally view the entire group. Consequently, they may choose someone who they weren't evaluating. I encourage lively conversations and lobbying for each evaluator's favorite candidate.

I have interviewed more than 4,000 people and hired several hundred using this format. Although I have no statistical study to show a lower turnover as a result of this process, I have experienced a lower turnover. I estimate turnover can be reduced by 20 to 30 percent using this interview format. Why? It's simple: you have more information on which to base your decision and, therefore, make better selections.

Some people wonder if I have ruined the process for future group interview candidates since I have written this book and exposed the process. The candidates may be more aware of the process, but they can't fake who they are for three-and-a-half hours. I have interviewed candidates multiple times in different group interviews, and they still behave as newcomers, primarily because the experiment dynamics change.

The Downside of the Group Interview

When you are interviewing in a group setting, you tend to grade on a curve. Consequently, that means that someone has to be first and someone has to be last. I have had group interviews in which my eighth-ranking candidate in one group is better than my top-ranking candidate in a second group. This is why you should develop a scoring sheet to rank all candidates based on the way their skills match the job needs. An example of a scoring sheet is in the Appendix.

The One-on-One interview

There is much written on perfecting the one-on-one interview, but since my company does a group interview, the one-on-one time should be a final blessing of the things you have already discovered.

The following suggestions might prove to be helpful. Save the responses the candidates gave during the first interview session and ask them the same questions but in a different format. See if their answers remain the same or if they were just playing to an audience.

I like to have three or four different people interview the person the same day and ask a couple of similar questions, again looking for consistency. The question could be as simple as "Why did you leave your last job?" See if the question when asked repeatedly elicits the same response.

Afterwards, interviewers should get together and compare notes. You will be surprised at how different interviewers can come away with different answers to the same questions.

One explanation might be that each interviewer's style elicits a different response or perhaps we as humans simply process information differently and may interpret the same information in different ways depending on our paradigms.

The one-on-one interview is always a great time to ask "off-balance" questions, things for which the candidate couldn't possibly prepare. The objective of these off-beat questions is to see how well people think on their feet and to get people out of the traditional interview mentality so their responses are less rehearsed. These questions also provide some fun during the interview process. As with the group interview, the one-on-one interview will give insight into a variety of issues that help you determine what the person thinks on a variety of topics.

Below is a series of predetermined queries designed to uncover whether your candidate has the skills and characteristics necessary to succeed in the available position.

The predictive nature of the typical employment interview isn't much better than randomly picking résumés out of a stack and hiring those people.

As organizations begin emphasizing team approaches to management and problem solving, selecting employees who best fit the culture and style becomes critical. Only behavior-based questions can assist you in selecting the right candidates.

Interview Questions That Work

Questions to reveal personality, temperament, and ability to work with others:

- If you had to describe yourself in three words, what would they be?
- How would you describe your personality?

- What motivates you most?

- What brings you joy?

- If I call your references, what will they say about you?

- Do you consider yourself a risk-taker? Describe a situation in which you had to take a risk.

- What kind of environment would you like to work in?

- What kinds of people would you rather not work with?

- What kinds of responsibility would you like to have in your next job?

- What are two or three examples of tasks that you do not particularly enjoy doing? Indicate how you remain motivated to complete these tasks?

- What kinds of people bug you?

- Tell me about a work situation that has irritated you.

- Have you ever had to resolve a conflict with a co-worker or customer? How did you resolve it?

- What sort of relationship do you have with your associates, both at the same level and above and below you?

- How have you worked as a member of a team in the past?

- Tell me about some of the groups you have had to get cooperation from. What did you do?

- What previous job was the most satisfying and why?

- What job was the most frustrating and why?

- Tell me about the best boss you have ever had. Now tell me about the worst boss. What made it tough to work for him or her?

- What do you think you owe to your employer?

- What does your employer owe to you?

Questions to reveal past mistakes, management skills and self-improvement:

- Tell me about a goal or objective in your last job that you failed to meet and why.

- When was the last time you were criticized? How did you deal with it?

- What have you learned from your past mistakes?

- Tell me about a situation where you "blew it." How did you resolve or correct it to save face?

- Tell me about a situation in which you had to abruptly change what you were doing.

- What one thing would someone tell me you need to improve in order to be a great employee?

- What criteria do you use in setting priorities?

- Imagine I am an old man on a mountain and I own the only trading store in the area. If you could trade one thing of which you had an excess amount, what would you trade for of mine?

- Tell me of a time when you had to work on a project that didn't work out the way it should have. What did you do?

- If you had the opportunity to change anything in your career, what would you have done differently?

Questions to reveal integrity, social conscience, honesty, and trustworthiness:

- What famous person can you most relate to and why?

- What do you feel is the most honorable profession in the world?

- If you inherited $10,000,000 tomorrow, how would you spend the first million dollars?

- Discuss a time when your integrity was challenged. How did you handle it?

- What trait did your mom or dad give you that you really like? Really dislike?

- What would you do if your boss asked you to do something unethical?

- If you could donate a million dollars to one cause, what

would it be and why?

- Have you experienced a loss for doing what is right?
- Have you ever asked for forgiveness for doing something wrong?
- In what business situations would you feel that honesty would be inappropriate?
- If you saw a co-worker doing something dishonest, would you tell your boss? What would you do about it?

Questions to reveal creativity, whimsy, creative thinking, problem solving:

- If you were an animal, what animal would you choose and why?
- If you were to rename yourself, what would your new name be and why?
- If you could choose your height, how tall would you be?
- What do you think was the greatest invention of humankind?
- If you were to build a city around a theme, what would the theme be?
- Tell us a joke.
- Persuade me to move to your city.
- When was the last time you "broke the rules" (thought outside the box) and how did you do it?
- What have you done that was innovative?
- What was the wildest thing you did in the past year?
- If you could do anything you want to do, what would that be?
- What is the most difficult decision you have ever had to make? How did you arrive at your decision?
- What type of approach to solving work problems seems to work best for you? Give me an example of when you solved a tough problem.

- When taking on a new task, do you like to have a great deal of feedback and responsibility at the outset, or do you like to try your own approach?

Miscellaneous Good Questions:
- How do you measure your own success?
- What is the most interesting thing you have done in the past three years?
- What are your short-term and long-term career goals?
- Why should we hire you?
- What kind of responsibilities do you want, and what kinds of results do you expect to achieve in your next job?
- What is the best thing a previous employer did that you wish everyone would do?
- What are you most proud of?
- What is important to you in a job?

Creative Reference Checking

When you can't talk to a candidate's current employer because he or she is still working there, you've got to get creative if you're going to uncover the strengths and weaknesses that candidate will bring to a new job. We are bound by rigid legalities regarding reference checking. In fact, it is difficult to get a former employer to give you a reference even on a stellar employee. People live in fear of the repercussions of saying something that may damage the past employee's reputation and are intimidated by the thought of litigation.

Reference checks are more to catch inconsistencies and red flags in a candidate's story. In general, you're not looking for incredibly glowing references or generalities. You're trying to determine a candidate's potential cultural fit with a company. For example, if leadership ability is a particularly sought-after skill, ask for very specific examples of how a candidate has used team-building skills to create focus, drive results and energize others to initiate real change within an organization.

I have gathered some creative techniques on reference checking from a variety of people. More and more people are subscribing to the philosophy of giving only the dates of employment, the job description and the person's title. Some employers are even reluctant to answer whether the employee is eligible for rehire. This allows you little insight into the performance of the person.

A friend of mine who worked for the state government was frustrated by the lack of cooperation he was getting from a fellow human resources director. He was trying to get performance-related information about a candidate he wanted to hire, but he was having no luck. All of a sudden, he came up with a different strategy.

"Look," he began, "I know you can't say anything about the person's performance, but I'm in a real dilemma here. I'll tell you what I'll do: I will count from one to 10, with 10 being the highest rating. When I get to the number that corresponds with how you would rate the employee, simply hang up the phone. You don't have to say anything."

There was silence on the other end of the telephone.

"OK, here I go … 1, 2, 3 …"

The telephone went dead.

Although you may not want to use this technique as your sole criteria, it still was a creative solution to the reference-checking problem.

Or call the reference during off-hours when you are likely to reach the person's voicemail. Leave a message saying: "If you think this candidate is worth hiring, please call me back." Of course, failure to return the call shouldn't necessarily disqualify the candidate, but it may be a red flag.

Don't just call the names on the list of references provided by the employee. Contact people not on the list who were likely to have had dealings with the applicant such as past supervisors, co-workers, and clients. Co-workers may not speak officially for the company, but they can speak from personal experience.

Business contacts outside the candidate's current company who have worked closely with the candidate, such as clients or customers, joint venture or project partners, and in some cases, vendors, can provide valuable insight. This is also the case with a candidate's former employer who has left the company, but can stress the candidate's importance within the workplace.

Colleagues from professional associations or other entities where the candidate's professional skills and performance might be known or evaluated are good sources as well.

Skill-Set Scoring

Have you ever had four different staff members interview the same person and all come away with different views of the same candidate? Why do you suppose this happens? We all tend to have our own little idiosyncrasies so we tend to hire in our own image. When I was a young manager in my 20s I tended to hire people to whom I could relate. Back then it was more like picking a friend than hiring a great employee. We all have our own biases about who we hire and don't hire. This type of discretion is okay to a certain extent but taken to the extreme the company needs are often forgotten. How do you protect against this bias? How do you develop consistency among the people involved in the hiring process? How do you hire to fit the needs of the company?

That's easy. Develop a list of what is most important to the company and to the position, weighting the most important skills and competencies. Every interviewer works off that list and rates the candidate on the preferred skill-sets.

Sit down with your key staff members and discuss the key skills for each position and rank what is most important for that position. If you are hiring a receptionist then a sparkling personality may be the most important trait, followed by the ability to deal with multiple tasks at the same time, followed by the ability to type. I usually list eight to 10 columns across the top of the page and then give each a weighted score. Then each staff member ranks the interviewee on a scale of 1 to 5 with 5 being the highest. You then take that score and multiply it by the weighted score and get an average for each skill-set. I have used this process hundreds of times over the last few years. I believe you will be surprised at how closely your staff members rate the candidate. Finally, total the scores across and get a total score for each candidate. This process eliminates a person getting the job because they blow everyone away with one skill, such as a great personality, and it allows you to focus on the total need of the job (see Scoring Sheet example in the Appendix).

I have been in groups where five different staff interviewed the same candidate with 500 potential points and the spread for the five interviewers was less then 10 points. A former executive with whom I worked introduced this system to me. It will help you develop a hiring culture that revolves around the true needs of your company.

Have fun with the process. Experiment with the types of questions you ask. Know what you are looking for when you ask the question. Remember candidates who are just being themselves and slipping into who they truly are, as opposed to interview candidates, can often deliver the most pertinent information.

Lessons Learned from Those in the Know

CHAPTER 8

Ralph Waldo Emerson must have had our service industry in mind when he wrote, "It is one of the most beautiful compensations of life that no man can sincerely try to help another without helping himself."

As I have said over and over in this book, some times our real compensation comes from things other than money and benefits. To further illustrate this point, I met with five chief executive officers of senior housing companies to learn their secrets of recruiting, hiring and retaining staff. Each of these top executives employs thousands of staff and faces tough challenges on a daily basis. Their messages are, at times, simple and consistent, yet creative and strategic.

Sunrise Assisted Living

Sunrise Assisted Living has grown to become one of the most elite providers of senior housing in the world. Paul and Terry Klaassen founded the company in 1981. The couple converted an old nursing home in Oakton, Virginia into a small personal care home with just a few beds. They borrowed money from their church and friends to make the renovations, most of which were done by the Klaassens themselves. Terry worked all day as the person in charge of care; Paul worked as a speechwriter by day and a maintenance man and caregiver by night. Their company now controls over 200 homes, and the company will produce estimated revenues of $450 million in 2001. They have over 12,000 employees worldwide and have been touted by *Business Week Investor* as the "Rolls Royce of assisted living."

I had the distinct honor of working for Sunrise for nearly five years. When I started with the company, it had 12 small homes after 12 years in business. I saw the company rapidly grow through private placement and the Initial Public Offering to over 60 homes during my tenure. The Klaassens taught me the importance of valuing each and every resident and treating them with the utmost dignity and respect. The company's mission-oriented approach to caring for frail elderly comes from the Klaassens and is sincerely conveyed on a daily basis. Terry and Paul walk their talk, which is very refreshing for a large publicly-traded company.

Their company has not forgotten its roots since being helped by their church in the early 80's. In speaking with Chairman and CEO Paul Klaassen, the philosophy and culture for the company was clearly articulated: "We are looking for people with a quality of heart, a mission orientation." Klaassen describes, "When we started the company, Terry and I recruited many people from our church."

Sunrise has an outstanding reputation as a company that puts the mission of caring for the residents first. You only need to look on the back of their business cards to recognize this important characteristic. It reads:

Principles of Service

- Encouraging Independence
- Preserving Dignity
- Personalizing Services
- Enabling Freedom of Choice
- Fostering Individuality
- Protecting Privacy
- Nurturing the Spirit
- Involving Family and Friends

"In the last 20 years we have seen the hiring process turn around. Employers used to interview employees; now employees interview employers," states Paul Klaassen. Sunrise has come up with a strategy that it feels has been successful for them. First they look to hire hearts. Klaassen explains, "That is to say, we hire people who have a strong desire to serve. These people will have basic character traits that we discover via the group interview process that allow us to evaluate their desire to serve.

"With regard to recruitment we aim to be the most flexible employer in America. That means allowing staff to choose their own schedules. We then evaluate this claim through our internal audits systems to see if we are living up to this claim.

"Our priorities in attracting and keeping staff are four-fold: We want people to know about our flexibility; we develop an

"In the last 20 years we have seen the hiring process turn around. Employers used to interview employees; now employees interview employers."

attractive physical environment for people to work in; we provide an attractive management culture — a place where employees are treated with respect and dignity; and we convey our financial strength to employees."

People have worked for employers where they have run into negative situations with regard to that employer's financial strength. This situation may result in a variety of negative outcomes for the staff person. By conveying their financial strength, Sunrise is really saying, "You don't have to worry whether or not we are going to be in business tomorrow or if you are going to be paid." That in turn translates into opportunity for people. The company is not only doing well but it is prospering. Consequently, people see the opportunity for advancement and promotion.

Klaassen, who is largely known for his progressive ideas, said he has developed a hierarchy for testing the character of employees. It is diagramed below:

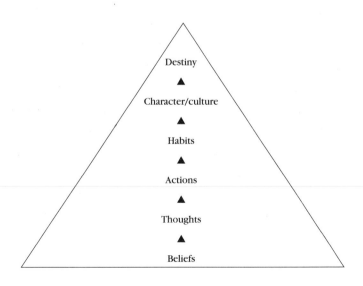

Destiny

▲

Character/culture

▲

Habits

▲

Actions

▲

Thoughts

▲

Beliefs

"Beliefs" serve as the foundation of this hierarchy. Klaassen is careful to explain that he isn't speaking in terms of religious beliefs. It could very well be that the type of volunteer work a person does helps to evaluate his or her belief system. These beliefs then translate to thoughts, which translate into actions, which become habits, which define character.

If you are a company, this same ladder will define your culture as opposed to an individual's character. This foundation will lead to your destiny. "When we look at people we have to look at their basic belief system." Paul Klaassen feels that a belief system can largely tell you how employees will affect people with whom they come in touch. According to Klaassen, that affect will be positive or negative. "I am somewhat skeptical about people's ability to just change their belief system. That's why most self-help books fail, because they try to take people from belief to destiny and skip a few steps."

Sunrise put an emphasis on hiring for the culture of the company first. "We make sure we are hiring for our culture and a set of beliefs first. We can train the technical aspect of the job; you can do the reverse."

Sunrise gets 70-75 percent of their candidates from the Internet and tries to make the application process an easy one. But the key to hiring, Klaassen insists, is to keep your good people. To that end Sunrise does a variety of things to sensitize management to the needs and challenges of their line staff. The first is a program called "Homework." Every senior management staff member, including the Klaassens themselves, performs a line staff function for two days. They actually bathe, feed and dress the residents —all duties required of a line staff member. This service helps to eliminate the barriers between management and line staff. It gives both parties an appreciation for the work that goes on. Line staff value the fact that management cares enough to come and work in the trenches.

Sunrise has also instituted a program called "Respecting and Honoring the Profession of Caregiving." This is a program the management has introduced to value line staff and the job they do in caring for the elderly. It is a program measured by internal auditors who look to see how care is provided. By doing this, Sunrise is, in essence, adding importance to the job of the caregiver. They are making a statement that the job is the essence of what they do. The staff in turn feels a sense of value for what they are doing and that they are not only important but also essential to the overall mission and objectives of the company. Klaassen believes we would all be better off looking for more youth workers and volunteer workers. In the end, people want to be part of something. They want to be "in the know." They want to be valued.

Sunrise seems to have the right formula. Their line staff turnover has gone from 85 percent a few years ago to 56 percent today. "At the end of the day, appreciation of an employee is valued more than a $.50 an-hour raise."

Emeritus

If ever there was a brainchild award for senior housing, I believe that honor would have to be bestowed upon Dan Baty, Chairman and CEO of Emeritus. Baty's career has spanned almost three decades in senior housing, including a stint as President and Chief Executive of Hillhaven Corporation at the ripe age of 27. A Harvard University-educated lawyer, Baty led the company's growth to over 400 nursing homes and nearly 30,000 staff members making Hillhaven one of the largest nursing home chains in the world.

Baty started Emeritus in 1993 by buying properties around the country. Within two years, the company had nearly 5,000 senior housing beds. In viewing the last 30 years, Baty says that not much has changed regarding staffing. "We have the same problems that we have always had — trying to get people to accept lower paying jobs and then keeping them. The turnover is still very high for the entry level jobs.

"I am not really sure how much we (senior managers) can do to affect this area. When I call a home that has not been doing well and then — all of a sudden — we see a surge in occupancy, the reason for their success is always the same. The manager hired the people with the right attitude.

"We have a work environment that satisfies some people, but not others. How do you explain long-term employees in this competitive economy? They like the environment, they like the team, and they like the work. You have to hire managers who bring enthusiasm to their job. Their personality is one that people are drawn to. These are people whose personal life is probably an indicator of how people are drawn to them. They will have lots of friends. This type of manager makes the employee feel valued and a valuable part of something."

Healthcare is an industry that is counter to good economic times. When unemployment is low, healthcare does battle for labor with other industries. When unemployment is high, people will gravitate toward this field. Consequently, the healthcare sector often does well when other businesses do not because of the labor factor. This is because healthcare is stable domestic work while other occupations such as waitressing are dependent on other influencing factors such as tourism.

Emeritus' strategy for hiring and retaining good employees is to emphasize customer service. "Good customer service starts in the corporate offices and then we convey the strategy that the field staff is corporate's customer. If we do a good job of servicing our customer (employees) in the field through the services we provide in the corporate office, then we feel that an attitude will be engendered on how the field staff treats the residents. Our message as a company is that we care about people — that is really the difference. If people feel that they are cared about, turnover will be less, your marketing will improve, and your profits will increase. People are drawn to this field because of their desire to care for people.

"I was always surprised by how many administrators we used to have at Hillhaven whose spouse had some type of disability. These people had a desire to care for people in all aspects of their life," Baty comments.

There is no magic to retaining people. Show them you care, involve them in what is going on, and make them part of the team is Emeritus' Philosophy.

"Good customer service starts in the corporate offices and then we convey the strategy that the field staff is corporate's customer. If we do a good job of servicing our customer (employees) in the field through the services we provide in the corporate office, then we feel that an attitude will be engendered on how the field staff treats the residents."

Holiday Retirement Corporation

William Colson of Colson and Colson/Holiday Retirement Corporation is one of the true giants in senior housing. In 1963, he and his father formed a construction company to build residential properties. In 1970, his company began focusing on the building and operating of retirement homes. Today, his empire includes 241 homes in North America in addition to 35 very high-end assisted living homes in France and 1,780 diversified projects in England. According to the April 2001 issue of *Professional Builder*, his company is the 82nd largest construction company in the United States. His various companies are responsible for more than 11,000 employees worldwide.

Colson describes his product as "Wal-Mart like" and something of a Chevy model that is affordable to most Americans. When asked about his philosophy of recruiting and hiring, his answers are swift and simple.

"Hire people that are over your head," he begins. "Hire people whose smarts scare you to death." He further recommends looking for people who are going to challenge the system and give the management the benefit of their brainpower.

When asked what he learned early on in his career as a manager, Colson responds, "I learned people were everything in this business. It is not the building you build; it is having smart people who can make decisions. Every person comes with some little trait. The job of a manager is to find out what that person does extremely well and let them do it."

Holiday Retirement Corporation does not offer incredible salaries or extraordinary benefits packages. Line staff must work 32 hours to receive medical and dental benefits, yet the company only pays 50 percent of the premium, leaving staff members with a $65-a-month payment for insurance. Staff members are not eligible to receive medical benefits until their six-month anniversary with the company, and their wages are described as "middle-of-the-road."

"What we do is create an environment for our staff and residents that is based on a grassroots campaign," explains Colson. "Our whole mission is based on the 'Touch Philosophy.' We look to hire people who have a high degree of passion for their job.

"We also teach the 'Holiday Touch Philosophy' which deals simply in the ability to make someone comfortable by giving him or her a hug or a pat on the shoulder," he continues. "We treat our staff the same way. People are called to our type of work because of what they do; they feel they are a part of a team that is caring for someone."

The company, of course, does have creative programs. For example, every two months it gives its live-in managers a "getaway allowance," granting up to $200 for a weekend getaway including accommodations and even RV rental or camping fees. This program allows managers to recharge and come back to the company refreshed and ready to go. The company also hosts meetings for management staff in locations such as Hawaii and organizes educational sessions as well as entertainment options.

The true magic, though, is really manifested by the company's environment. Despite the fact that the average retirement community may house 150-200 senior living units, staff is relatively small, primarily because of the live-in style of management. The low acuity with active residents diminishes the need for a larger staff. These properties are typically operated success-fully with 15 to 20 full- and part-time staffers. The beauty is that because of the small number of people, residents are able to bond with members of the staff more quickly and earn a sense of having a family: everyone knows everyone.

The proof of the management's success lies in the company's turnover rates. The annual manager turnover rate at Holiday Retirement Corporation is a low 24 percent. Even more surprising, 14 percent of the 24 percent are actually promoted within the company. It's not all a bed of roses, however. The turnover rates for live-in staff members is at 80 percent because, as Colson explains, "live-in management is not for everyone and typically people self-qualify and leave."

The amazing story is in the line staff turnover which Colson states is at a mere 50 percent, less than half the industry average. When questioned about the reasons for the low turnover, Colson again attributes the family/team atmosphere in the building and the fact employees are drawn to the caregiving profession. "We try to listen to people's needs and hire those who we can accommodate," he says. "We hire a lot of single moms who arrive at work once they send their kids off to school. We then allow them to work a schedule where they are off work by the time their kids get home from school."

As for recruiting, the company uses traditional newspaper ads but has seen a recent surge in recruits responding to Internet job boards, especially the Monster Board on Monster.com. Too often, when we can't reduce turnover or hire the kind of staff that we need, we think it is because of money or benefits. Holiday Retirement Corporation is a model that substantiates that the company culture and its treatment of employees is oftentimes more valuable than money alone.

Leisure Care

Leisure Care is the preeminent regional provider of senior housing based in Bellevue, Washington. I had the distinct pleasure of getting my start in senior housing with this company and growing up in this organization known for quality. Their culture is one that is described as being extremely professional. Leisure Care has some of the best training programs in the country but, more importantly, its hiring practices are some of the best. In my seven years with the organization, I was taught to look for people who had a passion for quality, no matter what position you were looking to fill.

The founders, co-chairs and owners of this privately held company are Chuck and Karen Lytle. Their diligence in hiring great people has allowed Leisure Care to dominate the market position in areas where they serve. When I talked with Chuck Lytle, he was very clear about why his company is a success: "It all starts with a culture, a place where people want to work. Once you have created that, it is up to the managers to preserve it when they hire people. Of course you have to be competitive in the wages you pay and the benefits you give, but in the end people will choose you because of your corporate culture and the way that philosophy is conveyed by the people who are doing the hiring."

They are not just filling a position. In a sense, they are creating a disciple of the culture. Managers, in part, need to be trained to convey the message, the philosophy and the mission of the company in a strategic way that attracts people. This is just a matter of conveying your best assets to the prospective employee and Leisure Care does this. Too many companies take a haphazard approach to this issue and don't convey the strengths that lie within the culture of the company.

Some large companies do it so well that prospective employees start doing it for them. You need only to think about cultures like Nordstrom or Starbucks to contemplate how companies have been strategic in this endeavor. There's no confusion about the difference between the promise and the reality. When you go into a Nordstrom or a Starbucks store, you notice warm, rich colors. Lighting is pleasant, not harsh. Music subtly sets the mood. Every interaction is tailored to your unique tastes and wants. It's not a typical transaction where you are literally just a number. Each staff person is an emissary of the company's image and philosophy.

They are not just filling a position. In a sense, they are creating a disciple of the culture. Managers, in part, need to be trained to convey the message, the philosophy and the mission of the company in a strategic way that attracts people.

A large part of the Leisure Care culture is having fun. Lytle explains that they try to incorporate this fun into their employees' day. They incorporate talent shows into management meetings, host karaoke nights, and they even turned a regional meeting into a camping excursion.

Dan Madsen was appointed company President and CEO in 1998 after working his way up the corporate ladder. Starting as an administrator in 1988, Madsen held several positions in the company. Madsen shared a unique insight about his company's struggle to meet the needs of staff: "Nearly three years ago we found ourselves coming into a staffing crisis. We were being very reactionary in hiring. We were not taking the time to hire people who enhanced our company.

"We got to a point where we managed by fear, so the company was reacting to every aspect of the employees' needs in an effort to keep them. We got to a point where we were just happy people took the job instead of seeking employees who embraced the company culture and were in line with the vision. This cycle lasted about 12 to 18 months for us, until we decided we really needed to go out and 'take our company back.' We were being taken hostage by employees.

"We decided the culture was appropriate, and we wanted employees who were excited by our goals. The managers of the company had to constantly go out and repeat the mission and vision of the company and not allow for our position to be compromised.

"Our goal was to continue to have a company that hosted a family environment as well as a fun environment. I went out and personally interviewed people from all positions and asked them for their ideas. We also looked at various communication devices to get more people involved with our culture. We now have an excellent newsletter that goes to our employees and has been very effective. We have also started the Leisure Care Learning Center that focuses on training for all staff. The training is not related to just business issues or industry issues, but to train other things the staff may be interested in. Our staff volunteers for skills in which they have expertise such as dog handling, and we host the training at each of our sites. Our residents can even get involved in the classes. This has been a great success and the employees feel very appreciated." Madsen says the programs have more than paid off. Leisure Care has seen line staff turnover go from 89 percent to 68 percent in the last year.

Leisure Care also tries to involve its employees in the management of benefits. Madsen described a scenario where an employee recently became very ill and ran out of sick leave. Fellow staff members asked if they could donate some of their sick leave to the employee. In an effort to be consistent with all employees, Leisure Care came up with a protocol for employees to donate a portion of their sick time to a sick time pool. Leisure Care matched the donation to the time bank. Thus, the company circumvents certain employees getting a benefit that others don't. This is a great example of a company providing for employee needs with a consistent policy.

"Although we think we are very progressive in how we allot benefits and compensation to people, the real reason people work here is because the owners care about them," Madsen asserts. "I just got back from a week's vacation and both owners gave me a hug as if I had been gone for a year!"

What the Big Guys Do

CHAPTER 9

Starbucks Corporation

Your first thought is you have just entered a chic art gallery in SoHo. Your vision is instantly drawn to vibrant colored murals. Catch phrases like "coffee, perfection for the palate," and a scene of energetic people buzzing around on hardwood floors creates an atmosphere in which you feel things are happening. You realize this is more than just an ordinary visual showcase. This is the home of the company that put words like "latté," "cappuccino," and "barista" into the average person's every day vocabulary and has people all over the world drinking out of cups with mermaids on them. This is the world headquarters of Starbucks Coffee.

The environment here is much more than just visual. It resonates with good vibrations. Staff members are dressed in comfortable clothes and are clearly enjoying themselves as they sip coffee from taster cups. There is a common dedication that is apparent. The company is creative and it has stamped this environment as its own.

The old office building that houses their headquarters has been transformed through the use of creative lighting and paneled walls. The result is a very upscale office space. Frank Sinatra's music settles over the rooms where staff members are lounging in overstuffed chairs. It becomes evident to you that part of the reason Starbucks has been so successful with their coffee house concept is that they know the importance of matching lifestyle environments to the people. This is validated a few minutes later when I meet Howard Schultz, Chairman and founder of the coffee company that has nearly 42,000 employees in 4,000 locations.

I'm escorted into Schultz' reception area where he warmly greets me. After exchanging pleasantries, I ask him what makes Starbucks a special place for people to work. "People want a company that is a reflection of who they are," he says. "We have tried to build an organization that reflects lifestyles. We have never said that profit and revenues were the main objectives. We work to build trust and confidence with our staff."

"But doesn't every company try to do that?" I ask. "What do you do that is special?"

"We spend a disproportionate amount of time talking about and teaching company values. Some people come to us with a high cynicism factor and bad habits. It is our job to gain their trust.

"When we started the company we called our employees 'Partners,'" he continues. "When we went public, we didn't want to leave any staff behind, so we gave stock options and a comprehensive health plan to all of them. This action was unheard of in an industry like ours and was a cultural change in the way people did business."

"What did this do for Starbucks' employees?" I ask.

"You should never underestimate or minimize the effects and action this (giving stock options) has on a person's self-esteem," he replies. "I have a file from employees telling me about the things they have been able to do because of our stock's success. Things like sending their kids to college, buying a home, or sending their parents on a trip back to their native land. We call our stock 'Bean Stock.' These stocks have allowed many people to own something of value for the first time in their lives. This stock ownership created a very special excitement and culture of people doing things together."

He explained further that employees are given a maximum of 14 percent of their base pay in stock that vests over a four-year period. Even with Wall Street woes, Starbucks' stock has stayed strong with a market cap of almost $9 billion.

You can easily conclude that Starbucks is a company that would be prosperous even if it didn't have the great success it has experienced in the stock market. Schultz is a leader who takes pride in his staff and their welfare and, even as the company swells with no end in sight, the founder remains grounded with his people. I ask him how the company keeps in touch with all its current and new employees.

Schultz offered the following opportunities for staff. Open Forums occur a couple times each year. All retail Partners in a given zone are invited. "Part of the agenda provides an opportunity for our Partners to ask whatever questions are on their mind. Zone Management Partners are present as a resource to respond to these questions. Manager Meetings occur weekly, typically by district and facilitated by a district manager. In addition to the planned agenda, the district managers use a 'What Board' to generate questions from their store managers. The 'What' question might be something like, 'What questions,

topics or concerns do you want addressed in our
meeting today?' "

Town Hall meetings occur about once a month in different areas in the zone. These meetings are smaller than the Open
Forums for the purpose of generating more discussion. The audience is usually held for shift supervisors and hourly baristas.
"These meetings give our Partners, who don't have as many
opportunities, the chance to voice their opinions, questions
and concerns. The meetings also demonstrate how much our
company values the opinions of the 'front line' and were instituted so that managers could have a better idea of what issues
are out there and then have the opportunity to address them."

The facilitators of the Town Hall meetings are not the
Partners' managers, thus allowing the audience to freely share
their thoughts in a confidential environment. Although the facilitators may come with a few questions to get the discussion
started, the rest of the agenda is open to the audience. "These
types of exercises keep employees plugged into the company,"
says Schultz. "We want to know what people have to say. We
will not hide behind the veil of corporate hierarchy."

Involvement outside the company is important, too. An
area of philanthropy Starbucks supports is literacy. The
Starbucks Foundation, a foundation started in 1997, has
awarded more than 400 grants totaling $3 million to literacy,
schools and charity organizations across North America. The
Partners champion local literacy programs through their volunteer involvement and sponsorship of literacy grants from the
Starbucks Foundation. This reinforces the power that people
can have and has a enormous impact on their self-esteem.

When talking about his employees, Schultz speaks with great sincerity and passion. You can tell that he has a great respect for them and a genuine concern for their welfare. This is evident when he relays the story about Kenny and tells it with great emotion: "I was asked to speak recently at an employee's 10-year anniversary. This employee has Down's Syndrome and is loved by everyone. He has truly touched many lives. A few immediate staff who work directly with the employee normally attend these kinds of parties, but Kenny's party had a packed house. Anyone who had ever worked with him was there to help him celebrate. This was a great example of celebrating the human spirit. Long-term profitability is not based on selling something; it is deeply rooted in values that people honor and that honors people."

Long-term profitability is not based on selling something; it is deeply rooted in values that people honor and that honors people.

And that is the essence of Starbucks. They don't just sell coffee — they sell an environment, a sanctuary from a crabby friend, an unkind boss, and a hectic day. Starbucks surrounds you with people who don't just process your latté order but offer you warmth and validation. Schultz is a genius at not just creating an environment in which its customers can thrive, but also a place in which Starbucks' staff can thrive. The reason the company turnover is less than 50 percent (in an industry that continues to experience staff turnover of nearly 300 percent) is because he has created a fun atmosphere, a place where people can contribute to their community, and a place that reflects the lifestyle of employees. Add to this, the fact that the company cares about impacting its staff's self-esteem and you have a winning formula for success.

Costco

If you have ever bought in bulk before, you have probably shopped at Costco, the wholesale giant. For years, I have been impressed by the wholesale chain's ability to keep customers coming back and filling their carts to the brim.

Jim Senegal, Jeff Brotman and Dick DeCerchio formed Costco in 1983. Senegal still acts as the company President and Chief Executive Officer. The company's world headquarters is based in the Seattle suburb of Issaquah, Washington, where it employs 4,000 corporate staff members. Worldwide, the company has over 81,000 employees in 346 warehouse stores. Costco did nearly $32 billion in revenue in the year 2000.

The employees have a tough job. There is a tremendous amount of heavy lifting that has to be done as employees move merchandise and re-stock the shelves. Additionally, the amount of customers in the stores make the customer service needs very high. People are in long lines at the checkout stand and, most often, the waiting causes stress to the customer. Employees must be able to make the customer feel good about the trunk load of items they will be purchasing.

With all these demands you would think that employees would have specialized training, recruiting bonuses, high start-

ing salaries and — still — employee turnover would be high.
Well, not so! Costco just does it better than most.

For many years, their annual turnover ran at a rate of 19-
20 percent. Their starting wage was between $8 and $8.50. In
2000, they saw turnover rise to 27 percent; still an incredible
success story considering turnover in similar retail operations
easily runs 50 to 60 percent. But 27 percent was not satisfactory
for the management of Costco.

John Matthews, Senior Vice President of Human Resources
and Risk Management comments, "We started to see our
employees leaving for jobs that were less physical and for
more money. Consequently, we felt it was time to up our starting wage to $10-an-hour. We feel now we have an extremely
competitive wage as well as an exceptional benefits program."
Costco offers medical, dental, disability, and Long Term Care
insurance, with no cost to employees who choose an HMO
and only a 7 percent cost for those who go outside of the plan.
Additionally, the company offers a 401(k) plan with several
different options.

But, if you ask Matthews, he would contend it is not the
salary or the benefits that attract and keep people. Instead, it is
the culture. "We feel you need a competitive wage and benefits
plan to attract people, but it is our culture that keeps people
coming to work."

When Matthews looks at the turnover at Costco he
segments when employees leave during tenure. How many
people left in the first 30 days, in the first 60, in the first 90,
and so on up to the first 180 days? "We feel the first six months
are critical in having an employee connect with the company,
so our goal is to have the employee connect with the company

as soon as possible. When we surveyed people who left in the first 30 days, it was because they had not connected with us as a culture. We found that 60 percent of the employees who left us in the first 30 days were de-selecting us. As tenure increases, turnover decreases. We found that the turnover rate for people who had been with us more than two years was only 11 percent.

"This told us we needed to put a greater emphasis on having those new employees connect with who we are as a company, what our culture was all about and the benefits of working for us. To do this, we knew we had to come up with a better idea than just have people sit in a classroom and give them propaganda about how great we are. Instead, new employees interview five members about what they like best about the company. Then they ask five fellow team members about what they enjoy most about the company. Not only do they get great feedback from people, but it also allows them to make the connection.

"Costco segments its training based on this method as well. We don't give all our warehouse people the same training the first day they come to work. Basic safety training is done initially in a few hours and then people are put on the floor to see how they work. The more extensive and expensive training is done with employees who have more tenure and whose likelihood of leaving is much less. Consequently, Costco turnover costs are much less — around $600 to $700 per employee compared with the average retailer whose costs are around $1,100 to $1,200 an employee."

Matthews also contends that there are three basic traits that make a good Costco employee: a person with initiative and hustle who can service a customer. "We knew that we couldn't train this in a classroom, so we assign a buddy (who is a veteran employee) to answer questions and we put the new person on the floor. We want our employees to make good common-sense decisions. We don't have reams of policies to assist them. We just ask people to obey the law and make good decisions."

The company takes a genuine interest in their employees. They almost exclusively promote from within. Matthews, who has a staff of 70 Human Resource and Risk Management people, says that almost all of his people came from the warehouse: "I don't have any people who came here who specialized in Human Resources. We want people who have real business experience." Many of the senior management team had modest positions in the warehouse retail industry, including Jim Senegal, who was a cart pusher with another warehouse company prior to forming Costco.

The company has developed Costco University, which has an ethics-based curriculum that conveys the spirit of the founders as to how they treat their fellow employees, vendors and customers.

"The company believes in constantly growing its troops and that means teaching and training of staff by the leaders in the company." Senegal professes that 80 percent of a manager's time should be spent teaching and training their staff. The company has developed Costco University, which has an ethics-based curriculum that conveys the spirit of the founders as to how they treat their fellow employees, vendors and customers.

"We also try to teach employees a way to say 'yes' within the boundaries of the law to these audiences. Our management staff does all this. We have very few specialized trainers in our company."

Costco has a very creative program that serves as a great economic incentive for the employee. Every employee that has 10 years of service or more gets a $2,000 check twice a year. This program was originally developed to deal with employees who hit the top of the hourly pay scale but needed a cost-of-living adjustment. But, it was such a hit with employees that Costco decided to initiate it for all employees. Employees with 10-to-15 years of service get $2,500, 15-to-20 years of service get $3,000 and employees with over 20 years of service get $3,500.

Costco employees can also rise quickly in payroll. The most highly trained and tenured employees are paid the most. In three years, employees can be topped out at a rate of $16.17 an-hour plus the twice a year bonus check. Over 60 percent of their employees are at the top of the pay scale. A cashier with three years of experience can be making between $37,000 and $38,000 a year.

But don't count on fancy soft benefits if you work for Costco. You would think that employees may get a bargain at a store that sells everything from doughnuts to tires, but employees pay the same for items as regular customers. Costco says that's because there is no fat in the pricing and the customer is getting the best price possible. Employees get a free membership card to the wholesale club, however. But again, it's the culture that keeps people.

Senegal encourages their managers as well as their boss and their boss's boss to share concerns in the employee manual. The company has an open door policy to address employee concerns.

"We take our employees' concerns very seriously," says Matthews, who said he recently received over 3,000 suggestions to the employee agreement. "We really value our employees. The company even has a Foundation that, although not widely publicized, is well-known. The Costco Foundation exists to help staff in crisis, people who lose a house in a fire, have catastrophic medical bills or other major life changing issues.

"We want to make an investment in our employees' lives," comments Matthews. The company takes this to heart. An employee who has more than two years of service can only be terminated by a Senior Vice President, and an employee who has five years of service or more can only be terminated by an Executive Vice President. "If we are terminating an employee who has five years of service or more, we as a company have done something wrong," says Matthews. "Even the President will know about these terminations. That encourages managers to do everything possible to make sure that their employees succeed."

Costco has done an incredible job of finding and keeping good employees. Although they have job fairs and great newspaper ads in areas where they are expanding, the majority of new employees either walk in off the street or come in by referral from a current employee. For a company that has an enormous population of line staff, they have still managed to keep their eye on how to connect with each and every employee. Their average employee stays four years and

10 months, enduring work that is both physically and emotionally demanding.

It is best summed up in Jim Senegal's address to staff in the Employment Agreement Handbook: "Despite the significant changes to our business, our goal is to maintain the atmosphere of a small company. One way we have accomplished this is by maintaining an Open Door Policy at all levels of our company. We urge you to share your concerns with your supervisor, manager, regional vice president or senior vice president as appropriate. You are not just employees to us. You are the people who help us run our business. We pride ourselves on having the kind of work environment where your dreams can come true with a positive attitude and hard work. All you have to do is set a goal and we will work with you to help you accomplish it."

Costco walks their talk.

Alaska Airlines

Alaska Airlines is a regional airline that has been around since the early 1930s. It started as an airline linking the Alaskan outback with the rest of the North American continent. In the nearly 70 years that have passed, they have become one of the more dominant regional airlines in the Western United States and have an outstanding reputation with its customers as being very service-oriented. With the same planes and destinations as most other airlines, Alaska knows the only thing that separates them from their competition is the interaction they have with each customer.

Alaska has nearly 12,000 employees and hires approximately 2,000 staff annually. Who wouldn't want to work for an airline, right? I mean, all that glamour, traveling to a different city, meeting interesting people.

"That glamour may be what attracts people initially, but it is not what keeps them," says Dennis Hammel, Vice President of Employee Services for Alaska. "The glamour soon goes away when people realize the work that goes into the job." The reality is if a flight is delayed, employees are dealing with an airport full of angry customers.

"What keeps our employees," points out Hammel, " are the bonds that people make in our company and the view that the company will take care of its people."

Despite the challenges, Alaska has managed to keep turnover down to under 20 percent for frontline positions. This is in an industry where the average turnover is hovering around 35 percent. A more staggering statistic is that the company's overall turnover, including management, is only a little over 9 percent.

So, how does the company get and keep their employees? Is it those glitzy travel benefits, great pay, and benefits? It is true the company allows each employee's spouse, child, parent and domestic partner to travel standby for free. The other benefits are standard medical and dental, as well as a 401(k) plan. The wages may be surprising to some people. A beginning flight attendant starts out at between $12,000 and $14,000 per year with flexible hours. Most baggage handlers, ticket agents and reservation clerks make between $8 and $10 an-hour to start. So the initial pay rate is not that much different than most other service-oriented jobs.

So again, what is the attraction? "We try to create a family environment that is fun," says Hammel. It's a statement a lot of companies espouse, but Alaska puts it into action. Alaska has gone so far as to have a recognition department. It has three full-time dedicated staff who do nothing more than recognize, motivate and create fun for the employees. These staff members plan holiday parties, random get-togethers, Burger Burns (hamburger BBQs) in the parking lot, and special recognition events. They are the ones who will search out and recognize the special employee who helped the little old lady upset about missing her flight.

"We look to create opportunities to celebrate being a family," says Hammel. "This department's sole job is to make sure that fun is being created. These types of events help employees bond with each other, make new friends and take a break from what may be a very stressful and hectic day."

The company is devoted to the group interview process and the dynamics it produces in order to determine if they are getting the right candidate. They set up mock scenarios to see how people will react with real-life situations. "Sometimes we get very attractive people, who by looks only you would think would make a great flight attendant, then after

We look to create opportunities to celebrate being a family. This department's sole job is to make sure that fun is being created. These types of events help employees bond with each other, make new friends and take a break from what may be a very stressful and hectic day.

they realize the work the job entails, they are not the best candidates," says Hammel. The company also places a big emphasis on having a variety of people involved in the hiring process. "The employee services and the hiring departments are involved in the hiring process, and either department may knock the candidate out of the running."

Five years ago, Alaska could place an ad in the paper and have the résumés just flow in. When résumés aren't so easy to come by, Alaska has an aggressive campaign to reach out to diverse groups such as Women in Aviation or the Black Pilots Association. "Our goal is to make the recruiting pool as large as possible and that means going to groups that would not normally come to us. We have to seek them out." The company also has success using its own Web site as well as other Internet services such as MonsterBoard.com, to recruit.

But the real success has come from the Employee Referral System. Alaska has a very unique program that goes far beyond paying an employee who refers a candidate. Alaska pays an economic incentive to the referring employee for assisting in the mentoring of the new employee. The longer the new employee is on board the larger the incentive. This incentive program could go on for as long as a year for each referred candidate. The company realizes that its greatest risk for turnover is in the first six to nine months; this program reduces turnover. Everyone wins. The company gets an employee who stays, the referring employee gets a bonus, and the new employee gets additional training.

"What we have found is that our veteran employees know our value system and job requirements, so they tend to refer very qualified candidates and then there is an economic incentive to make sure they succeed," comments Hammel.

The company also places a high value on its employees' input. In 1998, the company spent a year asking every staff member during an in-person interview what makes Alaska special. What resulted are the following Alaska Airline Values:

- Alaska Spirit (Can do attitude)
- Resourcefulness (Willing to help)
- Caring (a genuine desire to be interested in people's needs)
- Integrity (Do the right thing)
- Professionalism (Pride in who we are)

These values are then conveyed during the hiring process, in the initial orientation and in decisions that are made for the company. But again, Alaska does more than just talk about values; it models them by actions. Alaska will regularly re-route planes for a medical emergency in Alaska. These types of actions validate to the employees that they are working for a family-oriented company that cares. The company then goes to great lengths to listen to its employees from managers who have open door policies to various procedures that allow for more formal complaints. "We have to develop vehicles for listening and multiple avenues for expression that are safe for our employees," says Hammel. In an industry plagued with failure, the Alaska story is truly remarkable. It is no doubt that the key to their success is the people they have hired and the culture they have created.

Brown and Haley

If you have ever had the pleasure of eating the crunchy confection called Almond Roca, you have enjoyed a Brown and Haley product. Brown and Haley is an institution in the world of candy makers, a company that has survived the surges of mammoths like the Mars candy company. The company has been able to maintain market share and thrive. Founded in 1912 by the current Chairman and CEO Mark Haley's grandfather, the company will produce between $35,000,000 and $50,000,000 this year. The company employs approximately 230 full-time employees and experiences a 50 percent increase in seasonal staff during the year.

I interviewed the company because members of the business community in Seattle have commented about Brown and Haley's incredible history and longevity in a very competitive industry. What really intrigued me, however, was the family culture Brown and Haley has perfected. Brown and Haley also has an incredible record of keeping employees for a very long time.

I asked Mark Haley about the secret of his company's success. "We are a family-oriented company. People feel safe with us. We frequently have people who leave us and go work for much larger companies, maybe even for more money, and they come back because we treat them differently," suggests Haley. "I think there is something to be said for people who care about each other and know each other personally. They know that Brown and Haley is not a company that endorses the 'Last To Be Hired, First To Be Fired' philosophy."

Haley was asked to talk about some of his long-term employees and why they stayed. "We had a woman who came to work for us in 1920 and a gentleman who came to work for us in the mid-1920s. They met and eventually married. The woman worked for us for 35 years. The gentleman went from a line staff worker to Vice President of the company. After retiring with over 30 years in the company, he became a Vice President Emeritus and came to work every week until he died. His wife, now in her 90s, still comes to the office to visit. We became their family, their work family," comments Haley. Haley spoke of a number of similar stories including a night watchman who had lived in an apartment in the factory for nearly 50 years, and a current employee who is coming up on her 45th anniversary with the company.

Why do people stay? Is it the pay? Is it the benefits package? Haley said the average hourly wage is $10 an-hour. The company provides medical benefits for the employee and a dependent, plus a dental plan and a pension. But that's not the secret.

"This is a group of ethical people who truly want 'family members' to succeed. We invest in our employees' memories. That means

"That means we invest in their mistakes as well as successes. It is a lot harder for us to terminate a person in whom we have invested training than it is for a larger company. We go to extra lengths to help our people succeed. Staff knows this and they like knowing they are not just a number."

we invest in their mistakes as well as successes. It is a lot harder for us to terminate a person in whom we have invested training than it is for a larger company. We go to extra lengths to help our people succeed. Staff knows this and they like knowing they are not just a number. They appreciate their place of employment where it is safe to make a mistake."

Haley describes how the company was built on a foundation of caring and that his grandfather was a man of incredible sensitivity towards people. "He really cared for his staff, and his staff revered him for this quality. That has been passed down in the Brown and Haley culture. We care about one another."

It shows in the turnover rates. Turnover for full-time staff is less than 5 percent. "We almost see our lack of turnover as a problem because we can get stagnant when we don't have the fresh blood coming in." That's a problem most companies would love to have.

This attitude of caring is not just for current employees, but also for employees who retire from the company. Every year the company has a Christmas Retirement Party. They invite everyone who has ever retired from the company to lunch, a company update and a tour of the plant. "People love this event. Some people work here for years and are so appreciative to see people they used to work with and receive an update on the company. They really dress up. This is an event that some people look forward to all year round."

When Haley was asked why he did this for people that are no longer employed in his organization, his answer came after some pause. "We do so because we like these people. These people gave their lives to us. It is not hard to spend time with people you really like."

It is evident that Brown and Haley has perfected management simplicity in their approach. No fancy programs, complicated bonus systems, or big time frills. The company simply concentrated on creating a culture where people know each other, where staff feel safe to fail and where the owners of the company care and invest in every employee. So easy to say, so difficult to execute.

Bartell Drugs

Bartell Drugs is a business model for surviving in a big business world. The 110-year-old company operates a chain of 50 drugstores across the state of Washington. Bartell has managed to not only compete against the major national chain drug stores but has managed to flourish against them and continue to grow at a controlled pace, opening two to three stores a year. It is privately owned and employs nearly 1,600 employees.

I was intrigued by Bartell's lack of turnover at less than 20 percent in an industry that touts almost double that amount. During my interview with President and CEO George Bartell, I discovered that starting wages for line staff is in the $7 to $10 an-hour range. Benefits such as medical, dental, vision, prescription and life insurance are paid to employees who work a minimum of 100 hours a month. Obviously, the overall compensation package was nothing extraordinary. My interest grew to discover the secret of this company that existed since 1890 in a highly competitive world.

As I interviewed Mr. Bartell and Cindy Sankey, Director of Human Relations, it started to become clear to me why staff stay. "We really create a family atmosphere that keeps employees coming back, and that in turn relates to customer service. We try to do things that reinforce the goal of being a family-owned business," comments Bartell. Every year, the company sponsors a large family picnic. Last year's picnic attracted over 900 employees and family members. Each December, Mr. Bartell personally visits every store and wishes staff a "Happy Holiday Season."

The company also has a variety of venues to encourage employee communication. Regular employee roundtable meetings are held to give employees an opportunity to discuss issues that affect their success. Mr. Bartell also hosts "Lunch with the President," which is an event that recognizes special performers while at the same time allows staff to directly communicate issues with the president without dilution of the rank and file. Bartell also personally signs all birthday cards for his employees. It is amazing how little things like a birthday card from the president can have such an impact.

The company takes great pride in their customer comment cards that are placed throughout the store encouraging customers to respond. "Our customer cards allow us to recognize staff who do outstanding work during the course of their day," comments Ms. Sankey. "We then take time to acknowledge that person with an employee of the month award or a special letter from the president."

I pressed to find out what other things Bartell does that add to the company's success. I was waiting for something special, an incredible "Ah ha!" moment. As we spoke about the employees and the length of service, Mr. Bartell mentioned that the company employs an individual who has worked in a Bartell store for 43 years. I was interested to find out why someone would work for a company for that long and requested to interview the employee named Fran.

I interviewed Fran about her years at Bartell and why she stuck it out so long. She described her years with the company and the changes it went through. "I remember Mr. Bartell when he was a college intern in our store," Fran proclaims. I persisted with my questions about why she stayed with the company. "I guess it is just like a family for me, they are not a big chain and I like the fact that I know the owners of the company."

Still not satisfied with her answers, I persisted in my query to discover how Bartell is different from other stores, what do they do that no one else does.

In my quest to find some innovative technique, I had overlooked a simple human need — to be cared for.

"Well I guess the clincher for me was my surgeries," Fran offers.

"Your surgeries?"

"Yeah, I had a couple of surgeries and was in the hospital and both times the president took time out of his busy day to come and visit me, to ask how I was doing and see if I needed anything. To me, that is just like family."

In my quest to find some innovative technique, I had overlooked a simple human need — to be cared for. Bartell cares for his staff in a very personal way. It may not be with fancy programs, bonus systems or escalating compensation plans, but is done the old-fashioned way, by just caring for people for 110 years.

Vision Service Plan (VSP)

Chances are if you have a vision health plan, you are insured by Vision Service Plan (VSP). The company is an old timer in the area of providing vision plans. VSP was formed in 1955 in Sacramento, California. Since that time, the company has grown to dominate its field. VSP is as big as its five closest competitors combined. The company will produce $1,500,000 in revenue for 2001, has 2,200 employees, does business in all 50 states, and covers 33,000,000 people.

I had the pleasure of interviewing Roger Valine, President and CEO of VSP. Jill Mizuno, a friend of our Administrator in the Áegis office in the Sacramento area, suggested the interview. Jill works for VSP and informed me that the company had just been awarded the honor of being one of *Fortune Magazine's* top 100 companies to work for in America. In 1999, they were ranked 45 on the list and in 2000 they were ranked 19. I was excited to see what its recipe for success was all about.

I have interviewed a lot of people for this book: busy people, wealthy people, and important people. My interview with Roger Valine was one of the most down-to-earth and welcoming. It was very clear to me at the conclusion of the interview that Valine was VSP and vice versa. He lived the way he managed. Within a couple of days of making the interview request with his office, we were speaking on the phone like old friends.

In 1973, Valine joined the company straight out of college and worked his way up to President and CEO. But even though he is the head of the company, you can sense Valine has a great perspective on what it is like to be in the trenches.

"We have a company that is based on respect for individuals, values and beliefs, and an open door policy. We have great communication. I make it a point to tell employees the good news first and the bad news last. Some companies give this issue a lot of lip service but we practice it."

The company continuously trains on its value statement, which reads as follows:

In addition to our focus on the VSP mission and key strategic goals, there are other attributes of work at VSP that we believe are essential ingredients to our success and to making VSP one of the best places to work in America. These values are what we are committed to in our philosophy of doing business, our expectations and our standards of conduct. Our VSP values are:

- Superior quality service
- 'Can do' attitude
- Pursuit of excellence
- Personal integrity
- Treat others as you would like to be treated
- Teamwork

Ms. Mizuno told me that when she was first hired, she sent an e-mail to Valine thanking him for the opportunity to work for VSP. Within a day, he e-mailed back and asked if he could set up a meeting with her to discuss why she chose his company over others.

Valine has regularly scheduled talks with the employees where he gives employees good news and bad news. The company treats its employees as customers and puts its money where its mouth is by awarding 12.5 percent of all bonuses based on employee satisfaction.

VSP goes out of its way to create a company that is pro-employee. "I think we have a better environment than most employers out there. We try to think of things to do for our employees. We have a service for dry cleaning and a service to get your film developed in a day. But these are only the candles on the cake. The real essence of our success is in how we treat our people," comments Valine. The company is very devoted in its approach to please its employees with little things that speak to the caring attitude of staff.

For example, VSP gives out Christmas bonuses just like many companies (equivalent to one week's pay), but they give them to their employees in November. "We want to help our staff with the Christmas spending, and our staff loves it."

The company believes in having fun and gets together for a huge Halloween party where the president gives one of his annual talks and walks around and meets everyone. They also host a large formal ball in February where staff members come decked out in formal attire. "We are constantly polling our staff to see what we can do better. We have the expectation our staff is going to treat its fellow staff members as they want to be treated." The company believes in creating a family-based company, having a family picnic once a year and monthly cake day where all birthdays are celebrated. "One of the finest bakeries in the Sacramento area delivers 20 sheet cakes for cake day. It is a great event that gives people who don't normally work together a chance to socialize, get together, and bond with each other."

VSP is a firm believer in surveying. There are four primary constituents that it interviews. The first group are the doctors who use VSP's health plan. The second group encompasses the Group Health Insurance Companies. The third group is the actual patients who use the insurance. The last group, but certainly not the least, is comprised of VSP employees. The groups are frequently surveyed and results of these surveys are posted in the lunchroom for everyone to view. The company has even gone to the extent to name its survey department the "Customer Delight Department."

"We want to challenge our people to do a better job without sacrificing value so we reward for any innovation they may come up with. That way we are all aligned with what is most important to the company and we are working as a team to make it work."

The real key, then, is to link the company success with employee economic benefits. All staff have the same bonus plan: 12.5 percent of their bonus is focused on pleasing the doctors, 12.5 percent is based on pleasing the Group Health Insurance Companies, 12.5 percent is based on pleasing the actual patients and 12.5 percent is based on pleasing the employees. The other 50 percent of the bonus is based on administrative efficiencies. Staff can get up to one week's extra pay if they meet all bonus criteria.

"We want to challenge our people to do a better job without sacrificing value so we reward for any innovation they may come up with." Valine points out that senior management receives the same benefit as everyone else in the company:

"That way we are all aligned with what is most important to the company and we are working as a team to make it work."

The company offers all sorts of other incentives to its employees. It provides $2,500 a year for continued education. It also provides computer-training classes in which even family members can participate on a space-available basis. VSP has a terrific benefits package, but again, these things are not the essence of the company's success. They are mere tokens that further the company's caring philosophy.

VSP also makes it very clear the most important duties for an employee are the day-to-day performance issues. Every employee has what are called KJAs, Key Job Accountabilities. A person may have four to eight KJAs. Each KJA is ranked with the percentage of importance. For example "leadership" may be 45 percent of a person's KJA, with "vendor relations" being 25 percent. This gives employees the knowledge of how to spend their time and what areas are of special importance to the company.

Then the company translates these accountabilities into economic impact to the employee. Staff who score the highest levels on the KJAs may receive as much as a 10 percent increase in their annual raise. People are motivated to hit their KJAs and consequently the goals of the company are met and exceeded.

But again, money is not the driving force for people to work for VSP. In the company's annual survey, 32 percent of the staff ranked being treated with dignity and respect as the number one reason they worked at VSP. Only 2 percent said it was for money. The company had only a 14 percent turnover for jobs starting at $9.50 an-hour. But the more amazing statistic is that the company had 27,000 applications for 400 job openings. At a time when people are struggling for staff, VSP is not just a good example — it is a model.

The Essence of Recruiting

CHAPTER 10

Essence of Recruiting, Hiring and Retaining Exceptional Staff: 15 Points to Live By

Remember that at the root of every business challenge or opportunity is a human issue. Here is the essence of managing your employees and optimizing their potential. Through this simple philosophy you can transform your workplace.

1. Communicate everything you possibly can to your employees — good or bad — as quickly as possible without causing a negative impact on the operation of the company.

People want information; they want to be "in the know." There was once an incident when the media in Seattle, Washington, was tipped off that The Boeing Company planned to shut down a major plant. When the news was broadcast, Boeing immediately denied the rumors. Then, reports started to emerge that it might, in fact, be true. Employees were angry they were not told the truth. They were also incensed that they had not been alerted before the rest of the world. Share all information with your employees before the grapevine puts you in a position that makes you appear to lie.

2. Create an environment that endorses as much fun as possible.

Throughout this book, you've read it over and over again. VSP has their Cake Day and Halloween Party; Alaska Airlines hosts their Burger Burns. Good, loyal employees do not want boring, drudgery-filled work. There are many ways you can make work fun. It adds excitement and keeps attitude high and motivation up. Your employees spend an inordinate amount of time there, so make it a place where they want to go each day.

3. Be flexible.

Thirty years ago the employer would say, "These are the hours and these are the days off, take it or leave it." Those days are gone. The more flexible you are, the larger your potential work force will be.

Employee turnover can often be traced to work/life conflicts that can be easily and inexpensively remedied with flexible work arrangements. If a company does not offer part-time work schedules, telecommuting, compressed work hours, or some kind of other flexible work situation, an employee with child- or elder-care responsibilities may have little choice but to search for a company that does.

4. Treat every employee — no matter what position they hold in the company — with the same respect and dignity you would exhibit toward your favorite grandparent.

Remember back to what the line employees said they valued. People want to know that they are more than an employee; they want their basic human needs met. That is why Bartell Drug's employee Fran stayed with Bartell for 43 years. More than anything else she felt that she mattered, and that she was not just a replaceable part in a machine or system.

5. Know two personal things that are important to the employees you directly supervise, i.e., child or spouse's name, employee's hobby, pet peeve, favorite television show.

All employee commitment studies name touchy-feely attributes, such as care and concern, trust, respect and fairness, as essential to building loyalty.

People have a human need to be wanted. When a supervisor takes time out of his or her busy day to acknowledge something unique about a person it shows genuine interest in who they are. I was in a restaurant where I knew the manager. He introduced me to the waiter and said, "This is Joe. He is our nightshift waiter and — boy — is he an incredible gardener. He grows the best beefsteak tomatoes that I have ever seen!" The waiter blushed with pride and thanked the busy manager for his acknowledgement, clearly pleased that he was recognized for something beyond his professional duties.

6. Create a culture that every employee can describe with pride and enthusiasm.

VSP has taken this characteristic to the next level. Not only do their employees describe their culture with enthusiasm, but the enthusiasm is undiluted even two or three times removed from the employee. This is one of the reasons the company is so successful and has so little turnover. They have created a constant advertisement for recruitment. Conversely, if your employees are not pleased with their employment, they become a negative advertisement.

7. Share the wealth with aligned company goals.

It doesn't matter if you do it with stock options as Starbucks did, or with a progressive bonus plan such as VSP did, share the wealth with numerous people in the company. Try to give incentives to as many point-of-service employees as possible. These employees are in the trenches, touching and talking to your customers. No one wants to work for a company where just the top few people in the company are getting rich.

8. Give all employees the responsibility of making the company better.

This may seem like such a trite statement but too many companies have just a handful of senior employees responsible for the constant improvement of the company. To enlarge the scope of responsibility, you have to create venues of communication so that all employees can voice their opinion in a manner that is heard and acted upon. A dangerous protocol followed by many companies is to give people a voice without action. This inaction creates the old adage "It doesn't do any good to say anything. They're never going to do anything about it anyway."

Put line staff on committees and task forces to solve difficult issues. Put them in charge of their destiny with the company. This is also another way in which to say you value their insight and ability to work in a different capacity to solve this problem. You can create a great workplace showing trust through communication; sharing information on decisions and profits/losses; eliminating status and hierarchical differences; asking for help; and admitting errors.

9. Go beyond the norm in an employee emergency.

We are dealing with human beings. They have feelings, families, emotions and problems. Employers have a choice when these challenges occur. They can choose to pretend people aren't human and ignore the problem or they can exceed the expectation of the employee in an emergency. We often talk about how much we value our staff but the rubber meets the road when an employee has an emergency. All employees' eyes are upon you to see how you handle the situation. A light should go on that says this is a great opportunity to prove to my staff that I value them.

10. Create a physical environment that sends a message to your staff that you care about them.

We can talk and talk about how much we care about our employees yet we can't even supply a comfortable chair for them to rest their weary soles. Think about the environment your staff works in and how it may lead to greater efficiency. Think like a line staff member. Ask staff what items they would like to see in the rooms they commonly use. Offer resource information that has nothing to do with work but everything to do with challenges faced in day to day personal lives. It may be information on credit counseling or dealing with difficult teenagers or social service programs that may provide financial guidance. Be conscientious about building a comfortable environment for staff. Your staff should be your most valued customer, so take time to address their needs.

11. Look for services and programs from your vendors, customers and bankers that may enhance your staff's lives.

As business people, we come in contact with many people each day who have a variety of resources and talents. I will never forget the story my cousin, Patricia, told me about meeting Mother Theresa.

Mother Theresa asked Patricia, "Do you know where Chicago is?"

"Why, yes," my cousin answered.

"Could you and your friends send two dozen pairs of jeans in these sizes to this address?"

"Why yes, Mother, of course," my cousin stammered.

"Good, my child. Now, how can I help you?" Mother Theresa always had her customer in the front of her mind. She leveraged her relationships to get things done.

You as an employer have to adopt the same paradigm. When you meet with various audiences ask how they may enhance the lives of your staff. Always ask yourself whether or not there are additional opportunities to improve the lives of your staff. We are not looking for huge payoffs. It could be little things like dry cleaning at a discount or preferred seating at entertainment venues. The objective is to think about staff to encourage staff loyalty and retention.

12. Create a safe and personalized family environment.

There is one obvious common denominator when employee turnover is low: employees love their job. One of the reasons they love their job is that their workplace creates a very safe family environment. People are much less likely to leave a company if they have a good corporate family. As an employer, you can help nurture this process by facilitating fun events, sponsoring socials where people can get together, and recognizing the fact that if people have relationships with other co-workers, the chance of them leaving lessens.

13. Always hire "can-do" attitude over "can't do" experience.

We have all done it. The person has a great résumé that tempts our analytical side, but something just doesn't feel right about their attitude. You can always train skills, but you can't train attitude. These "can't do" mentalities have been the undoing for many companies and can bring down an entire team. Too many companies hire "can't do" experienced people and eventually it becomes the preeminent culture of the workforce. Shortly thereafter, when "can do" people are hired, they are quickly ostracized for being overzealous and a "do-gooder." The culture of "can't doers" quickly pressures others to conform or to quit. If you take over a troubled business, it may be worth the difficult process of "cleaning house" and starting fresh as opposed to keeping the experienced and hoping they work out.

14. Give your employees the incentive to recruit and an incentive to retain.

Alaska Airlines programs' are great at this. Not only do they give their people money to go and recruit someone, but they give them an incentive to get them through the first year when most turnover occurs. This mentality goes a long way in getting people to stay. A colleague has a vested interest in making sure the little things are done for the employee while the newness wears off.

15. Manage with vulnerability.

So often as leaders we want our staff to think we are perfect. The image of success has to shine from every pore. We are scared to show our flaws, so we over-compensate. We give the impression that we have everything figured out in all aspects of our lives. The problem is that people are more attracted to leaders who exhibit a vulnerability about themselves.

Remember how your favorite teacher in high school was the one who could laugh at the mistakes made, not the one who was perfect and rigid? This is the essence of a connection with people, especially line staff. I am not suggesting that you divulge very private matters in your life. I am, however, saying that it is okay for people to know about mistakes that you have made or issues with which you still struggle, maybe even issues you had growing up.

Why would you want to do that? Because you are dealing with people who are probably experiencing some form of these issues on a daily basis. When you, as the boss, convey your struggles to them, it gives them hope that they, too, can rise above their daily challenges to achieve a positive result. It allows them to connect with you in a very personal way that says, "Yeah, I've had that problem, too." This takes having great confidence in yourself and it takes practice.

Focus on the golden rule. Put yourself in the employee's shoes who might be asking themselves the following questions: Do people ask me how I'm doing? Would the company help if I had a personal emergency? Does the company provide family-friendly benefits? Do people pay attention to how I feel at work? Is the company developing me for the long-term, not just for the current job?

This book did not endeavor to find some previously elusive magic formula for retaining great staff. There is no single formula. Your formula will need to be found by you; customized for your unique company. However, the intimate perspectives generously shared here by some of this country's most dynamic companies has no doubt stimulated your thinking.

Viewing one's employees as the most valuable asset a company has is the central theme unifying all their stories. Each company story depicts leadership who sincerely believe that their success can only be obtained when their employees feel acknowledged for their intrinsic value. Each story describes leadership that sought, and sometimes courageously broke from traditional business school dogma, to find creative approaches to ensure that employees feel valued daily as individually vital within the team effort.

You now have a plethora of ideas on how to recruit, hire and retain quality staff. But, perhaps the first and most crucial act in which you can engage is to sit down with all levels of your staff, and simply listen. Take the time to understand their needs; take the time to see the world through their eyes. It will serve you well. Because, in the end, we all have a "Potato Soup" story to tell.

— **Glenn Hammel, Ph.D.**

Appendix

Hiring for Success Tool Kit

This tool kit is the key to finding great employees. Because your performance goals and rewards depend on finding qualified people fast, you don't have time to waste on activities that don't produce results! The sourcing funnel depicted below illustrates the process and its measures. The process involves getting a constant flow of qualified candidates into the funnel so that you can hire the most qualified candidate.

Measures

Meeting targeted organization-planning goals

- Meet projected quarterly timelines/goals
- Hire projected number of qualified candidates

Cycle time

- Measured from the date you started sourcing for a position to the date the candidate is on board

Note: this time can be reduced when qualified candidates are found at the beginning of the cycle by using the appropriate sourcing method(s)

Turnover (voluntary and involuntary)

- Measures overall organizational effectiveness
- Calculation: (Acquire data from payroll information)

$$\frac{\text{Number of staff members terminated for any reason during a period}}{\text{Average total staff members during period}}$$

Employment offer rate

- Ratio of offers made to number of applicants per position
- Measures overall effectiveness of sourcing methods/techniques
- Calculation:

$$\frac{\text{Number of offers of employment made per position}}{\text{Number of applicants per position}}$$

Notes:

Human Resources will set the cycle time and turnover standards on quarterly and annual bases.

Hiring for Success Process Flow

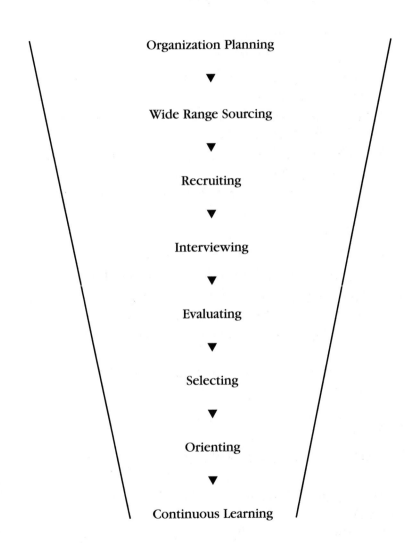

Organization Planning

▼

Wide Range Sourcing

▼

Recruiting

▼

Interviewing

▼

Evaluating

▼

Selecting

▼

Orienting

▼

Continuous Learning

Recruiting Steps (post sourcing)

Schedule new staff member for orientation.

Candidate accepts job offer.

- Personally contact candidate.
- Send follow-up letter with start date, salary/wage, and new staff member paper work.
- Be sure to remind candidate to complete paperwork prior to first day of employment.
- Notify community about new staff member including start date and position.
- Encourage staff members to welcome new staff member.

Evaluate and select candidates.

- Use the "Candidate Evaluation" form (p. 182).
- If candidate is a "yes," offer the candidate the job.
- If candidate is an "almost yes," wait to hear from "yes" candidate as to whether they accept the job.
- If "yes" candidate does not accept, offer job to "almost yes" candidate.
- If candidate is a "no," send a "thanks, but no thanks" card or letter.

Conduct interviews

- Use the "Four Question Interview" (p. 180).

Schedule qualified candidates for a group or one-on-one interview.

- Let candidate know who they will be interviewing with.
- Send out pre-packet letter or postcard confirming the interview date and time.

- Design interview based on the job qualifications necessary. Be sure to use the same interview questions for each candidate.

Implement your wide-range sourcing strategy.
- Track all candidates.
- Encourage candidates to apply in person.
- If in person, screen applicants on the spot.
- If application or résumé, screen as they come in.

Complete a position profile for the position(s) you are seeking to fill.
- Develop your wide-range sourcing strategy.
- Develop your company's compelling "story."
- Complete your organization planning analysis (below).

Organization Planning Worksheet

On the following page is an example of the first two quarters of an organization planning worksheet.

	Quarter 1				
Position	Beginning of Q1, # currently in position	Projected to add for Q1	Actual hired (+) or eliminated (-) in Q1	Number in position at end of Q1	Net Change for Q1
Care Manager					
Housekeeper					
Maintenance Director					
Marketing Director					
Assisted Living Director					
Life's Neighborhood Director					
Health Services Director					
LVN/LPN					
Activities Director					
Medication Care Manager					
Culinary/ Dishwasher					
Other					
Column Totals					

If actual hired is different than projected to add or eliminate, explain this variance.
If net change is different from actual hired or eliminated, explain this variance.
If year to date variance is more or less than zero, explain this variance.

Position	Quarter 2				
	Beginning of Q2, # currently in position	Projected to add for Q2	Actual hired (+) or elimi-nated (-) in Q2	# in position at end of Q2	Net change for Q2
Care Manager					
Housekeeper					
Maintenance Director					
Marketing Director					
Assisted Living Director					
Life's Neighborhood Director					
Health Services Director					
LVN/LPN					
Activities Director					
Medication Care Manager					
Culinary/ Dishwasher					
Other					
Column Totals					

If actual hired is different than projected to add or eliminate, explain this variance.
If net change is different from actual hired or eliminated, explain this variance.
If year to date variance is more or less than zero, explain this variance.

Classified Ad Boiler Plate

Classified Ad Components	Your Text to Use in Creating Your Ad
Offer — What will your company provide to the new staff member? (This should be something compelling).	
Target Candidate	
Primary Message	
Doing — What will the staff member do in his/her new position?	
Having — What skills, experience must the new staff member have?	
Required text	Apply in person. Contact information. Diversity, EEO statement.
Headline — This should be something compelling to attract a potential candidate's attention. You want the candidate to identify with your open position.	

Now, use this information to craft your ad.

Position Profile / Job Preview

Position: _____ Date Completed:_____

A Position Profile/Job Preview helps you anticipate candidates' questions about what a position or job is really like — what the staff member will be expected to do. Additional benefits of a Position Profile/Job Preview include:

- Showing that you're an organization of integrity in being up-front;
- Revealing those candidates who won't fit the profile;
- Preparing potential staff members; and
- Giving candidates an opportunity to "touch and feel" the community.

1. What are our staff member differentiators? What makes our staff the best?

2. Why would a staff member choose our organization? What makes us the "employer of choice?"

_____

_____

_____

3. What are the three top principal accountabilities for this job?

a) _____

b) _____

c) _____

Strengths of the position /Factors that make the job desirable:	Challenges of the position / Factors that make the job undesirable:
Note: During the interview you should be prepared to "sell" the various strengths of the position and why you are the "employer of choice."	Note: Challenges of the positions are potential objections or concerns. You should be prepared to overcome these objections or concerns if raised by the candidate.

The Four Question Interview

Candidate: _____

Interviewer: _____

Position: _____

Date: _____

Question 1: Please describe your most significant accomplishment or please tell me what you are most proud of.
Ask the candidate about his or her last two or three jobs and listen for personal energy and impact. Use fact-finding to get lots of examples and details — when, how, why, impact, results and time frame. Measure the trends over time.

Question 2: Tell me about your most important team accomplishment, or about a great team you have been on. Look for team work and/or team leadership during the last two or three jobs. Get examples of the candidate's actual role, time and effort involved, interpersonal challenges and motivation, and conflict resolution skills.

Question 3: One of our key principal accountabilities for this position is _____. Tell me about a time when you did something similar. Look for job-specific competency and get the details to minimize exaggeration. Anchor each major principal accountability with a past accomplishment.

Question 4: If you were to get this job, how would you go about implementing and organizing _____ (describe project). Look for adaptability and ability to contribute in a new environment. Ask about the top two or three principal accountabilities.

Candidate Evaluation

Candidate: _____ Interviewer: _____ Position: _____ Date: _____

Trait/Factor	1 - Very Weak	2 - Weak	3 - Good
Energy, drive, initiative	Little energy shown in any previous job. Passive work performance.	Generally consistent performance, but never exceeds expectations.	Consistent level of good performance with some high-energy periods.
Trend of Personal Growth and Performance Over Time	Growth trend is spotty. Inconsistent with basic needs of the position.	Trend of growth is spotty, but candidate meets basic needs of the position.	Trend of growth has flattened, but still consistent with needs of the position.
Comparability of Past Accomplishments	No job needs are directly met. The gap is too wide to overcome.	Only one or two Principal Accountabilities are met. Too many voids to overcome.	Key Principal Accountabilities are met with some voids that can be addressed.
Experience, Education and Industry Background	Weak fit on all standard measures: not enough experience or education.	Adequate experience, education. A stretch to meet minimum standards.	Solid education and experience consistent with needs of position.
Problem Solving and Thinking Skills	Structured thinking. Inability to adapt knowledge to new situations.	Some ability to upgrade and modify existing methods and processes.	Able to understand basic issues and come up with some alternative solutions.
Overall Talent, Technical Competency and Potential	Little direct technical competence or inability to learn within short time.	Some technical ability/talent but will take too long to come up to standard.	Solid. Technically competent. Good ability to learn. Some concerns remain.
Administrative, Management and Organizational Ability (people and/or projects)	Little relevant management, organization experience or unable to organize similar projects.	Some management, organization ability, but insufficient to make contribution soon.	Reasonable level of management, organization ability, but will have to grow to be more effective.
Teamwork, Team Leadership: Ability to Persuade/Motivate Others	Little evidence of persuading or leading others. More individualistic.	Some evidence of team skills, but inconclusive. More individualistic.	Solid teamwork, team leadership skills or potential, but not completely tested.
Character – Values, Commitment, Goals	Questionable values and integrity. Self-serving. Misleading.	Reasonable solid values and ethics, but questions remain regarding candor.	Appropriate values and ethics. No significant problems or unusual strengths.
Personality and Culture Fit	Fatal flaw or some imbalance or poor attitude and fit with existing team.	Adequate fit, but could cause some conflict. Might have negative impact.	All around solid person. Will fit with group without causing conflict.

Trait/Factor	4 - Strong	5 - Very Strong	Score
Energy, drive, initiative	Overall highly motivated, with a few brief periods of average motivation.	Consistent high energy, self-starter. Always exceeds expectations.	
Trend of Personal Growth and Performance Over Time	Strong upward trend of growth, and meets most needs of position.	Very strong upward pattern of growth, and meets/exceeds needs of position.	
Comparability of Past Accomplishments	Majority of Principal Accountabilities are met. Will learn rest quickly.	All Principal Accountabilities are met with strong past accomplishments.	
Experience, Education and Industry Background	Direct education and experience clearly meets current job needs.	Very strong comparable experience with good industry and educational fit.	
Problem Solving and Thinking Skills	Has ability to understand key issues and develop new solutions.	Understands issues completely. Can develop new creative solutions.	
Overall Talent, Technical Competency and Potential	Technically strong, insightful, quick learner. Broader focus.	Very talented, learns quickly, strategic, tactical and technical focus. Very broad.	
Administrative, Management and Organizational Ability (people and/or projects)	Solid management, organization skills. Meets all the needs of the position.	Has strong ability to manage and organize similar or larger type and size groups or projects.	
Teamwork, Team Leadership: Ability to Persuade/Motivate Others	Very strong teamwork, team leadership, but with some modest reservations.	Has very strong ability to motivate and develop others. No reservations.	
Character – Values, Commitment, Goals	A very committed person. Strong character, values, and attitude.	High integrity, very committed person with strong values and ethics.	
Personality and Culture Fit	Positive attitude. Personality will help in performance of job.	Strong, balanced ego. Positive attitude. Flexible and can work with others.	
Total Point Score		Score (Total x 2)	

Sample Executive Director Evaluation

Staffing and Retention

Candidate		Hire Great	Marketing Skills	Appropriate Business Background - Health / Hospitality	Polished Image / Articulate / Intelligent / First Impression	Entrepreneur / Innovative / Flexible	Implementor / Detailer (2, R)	Culture Fit / Pro-company / Motivator	Leadership / Management / Supervisory Experience	Communication Skills (1, 2)	Total Points
1	Candidate (score 1 - 5)	3	4	5	2	5	3	4	2	3	
	Weighted Score	15	13	11	9	5	11	12	15	9	
	Total -	45	52	55	18	25	33	48	30	27	333
2	Candidate (score 1 - 5)	3	5	4	2	3	3	4	4	4	
	Weighted Score	15	13	11	9	5	11	12	15	9	
	Total -	45	65	44	18	15	33	48	60	36	364
3	Candidate (score 1 - 5)	4	4	4	5	1	5	2	2	2	
	Weighted Score	15	13	11	9	5	11	12	15	9	
	Total -	60	52	44	45	5	55	24	30	18	333
4	Candidate (score 1 - 5)	4	5	5	5	4	3	4	3	4	
	Weighted Score	15	13	11	9	5	11	12	15	9	
	Total -	60	65	55	45	20	33	48	45	36	407

400	– ↑ –	Excellent
375	– 400 –	Very Good
325	– 375 –	Good
300	– 325 –	Fair
300	– ↓ –	Unacceptable